GU01018270

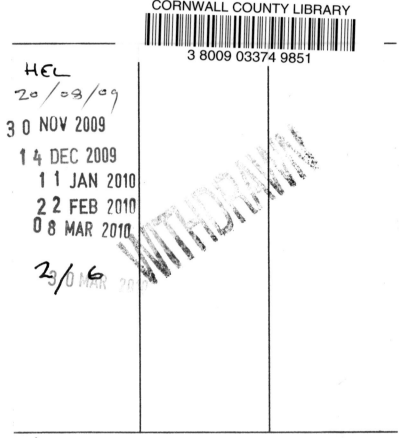

For my grandchildren
Ross, Kate, Megan and Chloe

Cadgwith and Poltesco

Once 'twas serpentine and fish ..

MICHAEL TANGYE
'Whythrer Meyn', Bard of the Cornish Gorseth

Federation of Old Cornwall Societies

Published by the Federation of Old Cornwall Societies 6 The Terrace Pentewan St Austell Cornwall

ISBN 0 902660 34 9

Illustrations by the author
and Barrie Yelland

Typeset by Susan Knight
Printed by R Booth Ltd, Mabe Penryn
© 2007 Michael Tangye

Cadgwith and Poltesco

Once 'twas serpentine and fish..

MICHAEL TANGYE
Federation of Old Cornwall Societies

ACKNOWLEDGEMENTS

My grateful thanks are due to the following:

The staff of the Cornwall Record Office for access to the various Hawkins Estate documents and the tithe maps of Grade and Ruan Minor; Angela Broome and the late Roger Penhallurick of the Courtney Library, the Royal Institution of Cornwall, for the use of the Charles Henderson records and contemporary Cornish newspapers; the staff of the Cornwall Centre, Redruth, who have cheerfully made available census reports, directories, contemporary newspapers and the illustration on which the book cover is based; Jonathan Holmes of the Penlee House Museum, Penzance, for permission to use photographs from the Private collection of the Penlee House Photographic Archive which appear in the chapter on Poltesco and its serpentine industry; the late Cadgwith residents Henry Jane and Richard Redvers Arthur who provided much information about Cadgwith in the early twentieth century, and are also acknowledged in the foreword; Anthony Hitchens Unwin for the loan of the 'Grade Survey Book', for access to Poltesco Mill, and for information imparted; Dr Oliver Padel who translated certain place-names; and those Cadgwith residents who provided information: Messrs B Bolitho, T Goddard and R Mitchell, Mesdames Irene and Jocelyn Jane, and D Law; and Gerald Luke , Frank Gibson of Scilly and Jocelyn Jane for the loan of photographs.

I must also thank Susan Knight for so patiently typing the text from my original manuscript, and Terry Knight, Deputy President of the Federation of Old Cornwall Societies, for overseeing the production of the book.

The appearance of any book is so important, and here I must again thank my old friend, Barrie Yelland, graphic designer and illustrator (pre-computer), for spending so many hours with me planning the general layout, designing the book cover, improving old photographs, and for his imaginative ideas in enhancing otherwise uninteresting maps, etc.

Michael Tangye
Redruth

Front cover: Coastal schooner, Cadgwith Cove.

CONTENTS
Acknowledgements
Foreword

FOREWORD

Of all the beautiful locations in Cornwall, Cadgwith remains unique. Always remote, a once tightly-knit Cornish community shut away from the world existing beyond the confines of its valley, it remains physically a typical example of many Cornish villages of the past. Its growth greatly accelerated from 1780 onwards, when the Hawkins family of Trewithen purchased the Ruan Minor half of the cove and invested heavily in expanding the pilchard fishery conducted there.

During the Victorian period its isolation ensured that little news of its activities reached the Cornish press, and like other fishing coves its interest was overshadowed by the larger fishing ports of St.Ives, the Mount's Bay etc. In 1972 this writer commenced an unhurried, ongoing study of the fishing coves of The Lizard and the Land's End peninsulas; at that time several elderly Cadgwith men regularly occupied the Stick, the wooden plank which served as a seat outside the then derelict Square Cellar, now the Old Cellars Restaurant. There they watched the tide come and go and reminisced of the days of their youth. Amongst them was Henry Jane, an ex-coxswain of the Cadgwith lifeboat and his cousin Richard Redvers Arthur, known affectionately as "Buller". From both I was to learn so much of life in the cove in the earlier years of this past century – the names of the various pilchard seining companies which operated there, the names and functions of the capstan houses, lofts, and fish cellars, many now converted to dwellings, anecdotes about characters of the past, place names, and dialect.

Sadly both Henry Jane and Richard 'Buller' Arthur have now passed on, but we should be ever grateful to them for recounting so much, which is contained in this modest history of their village. This study gave an opportunity to not only reveal the growth and life of Cadgwith, but chiefly to describe the working process of the pilchard seining industry, directly relating it to the people and buildings themselves.

As no visit to Cadgwith is complete without walking to Poltesco and Carleon Cove, a description of that enchanting valley, where its ancient fish cellar was replaced with a serpentine factory, is included.

DWELLINGS AND PEOPLE

The ancient fishing village of Cadgwith lies on the Lizard Peninsula at the seaward end of a small, steep-sided valley. Earlier forms of its name Porthcaswith in 1360, and 'Porthcaswyth' in 1542, can be translated from the Cornish as 'The landing place of the thicket' which was probably an apt description of the valley in medieval times. The 'Porth' was later dropped, leaving 'Caswyth', and 'Port Cadgwith' and now simply Cadgwith. [1.] During the seventeenth and eighteenth centuries the Robinson family held considerable property in the parishes of both Grade and Ruan Minor; the Rev. Thomas Robinson, who died in 1814, was the rector of the latter and George Robinson was its patron in 1702, owning a residence at Cadgwith which at that period was known as 'Robinson's Cove'.[2]

Today its huddle of picturesque thatched cottages is divided by a stream which flows into Cadgwith Cove, forming the boundary between the parishes of Ruan Minor to the east and Grade to the west, its parishioners known as 'Ruan Ducks' and 'Grade Geese'. The stream was covered when the lifeboat house was built in 1867, but before

that date it was spanned by a little wooden bridge over which people passed from 'Grade side' to 'Ruan Minor side'[3] as the two halves of the cove were known. Above lies the churchtown of Ruan Minor with its ancient church site dedicated to the Celtic Saint Rumonus, or Rumon (Ruan), but almost completely rebuilt in 1855. Here too is the still active Association Methodist Chapel and school amidst a mixture of thatched cottages and unblending modern bungalows.

Viewed from above Cadgwith appears as a virtual sea of thatch, protecting cottages built with serpentine, stone and cob. Serpentine was easily obtained from quarries along nearby cliffs and stone was dug from small quarries in the hillsides; one at

Church of St Rumon, Ruan Minor

9

Man-o-War Walk was last worked in 1914 for road metal stone.[4] (The name *Man-o-War* is probably a corruption of either the Cornish *Menavaur* meaning 'great rock' or of *Mainward Field* mentioned in 1793.) Timber for roof construction was frequently obtained from shipwrecks.

Much building occurred at Cadgwith between 1780 and 1800 when the new landowner of the Ruan Minor side, Christopher Hawkins, of Trewithen, leased a number of plots, including those adjoining Barn Hill which leaves the village on the east side. The quaint thatched cottages there at that time still survive, alongside one, The Cot, an earlier dwelling of the seventeenth century which now comprises of two cottages converted to one. In 1782 John Randle leased a dwelling house already there *"wherein Grace Luddra, otherwise Roberts now lives"*. It was 11 feet long and 16 feet wide. John was allowed to enclose a garden plot and rick place from a field called the 'Hill' behind the house. He also leased *"John Jacka's house"* there, 20ft long and 16ft wide, *"wherein Jane Thomas lives"* (see plan) and made a similar enclosure with space for a furze, or gorse, rick.[5] At the same time Peter Willey *"Yeoman"* leased a *"Dwelling-house now a barn or workshop, being Grace Luddra's higher house"*, next door to lower house.[6]

In the area now behind the Cadgwith Hotel, mariner Samuel Thomas built a dwelling house in 1783 *"next below a dwelling house called James Smith's house, 25ft 6ins long outside, and 14ft wide within the walls, with liberty to enclose a garden plot*

Transcript from original document
Key to plan, undated, possibly 1770-1780 (CRO).
"The Village of Cadgwith in Ruan Minor"

1.	Jane Thomas's House.
	d45 Three cornerd Garden.
	2. Lower walk Garden.
2.	Samuel Thomas's House.
	b3 higher garden on ye Clift..
	a29 Middle walk garden.
3.	John Randle's House.
	1 Garden under ye Mowhay adjoing. Middle Walk garden.
4	Garden to be taken out of the lower part of the meadow. Noᵈ c13 next ye mowhay.
4.	Jaˢ Randles new Stables.
	n13 half this mowhay to be allotted as a garden.
5.	John Hitchens's House.
	n13 half this mowhay to be allotted as a garden.
6.	Capstand House & Dwho – ye dwhouse only belong to James Randle.
7.	John Johns House. Garden allotted to do.
8.	Grace Luddras Higher House. Garden allotted to do.
9.	Grace Luddras lower House, Garden allotted to do.
10.	Smiths House. Garden allotted to do.
45a.	Great House. Garden allotted to do.
	c 4 corner'd Garden
	f Middle reens
	e Orchard

38a.	Dwho. & garden.	a13.	Dwelling House late Smiths.
	b. Park todden.		
	c. Long close.		
	d. The hill.	b	Orchard.
	e. Park todden Garden.	c	Meadow.
		n	Mowhay.

This part of the Tenement of Treworder-woollas, rent by John Randle.

: These dots denote two Stables built under the wall of the 4 cornerd Garden on the hill behind the house."[7] John Williams, a yeoman, lived in a *"newly-erected"* dwelling house in 1793 *"next below the dwelling house built by Samuel Thomas"* and created a garden plot behind *"on the hill as high up as the road and length of the house, and all those two gardens called 'Three cornered garden' and the 'Lower walk garden'"* (situated behind Old Cellars restaurant).[8]

James Randle, another yeoman, son of John , in 1786 *"lately built a dwelling house in the Port of Cadgwith 20ft 3 ins long and 16ft 2in wide"*, and created a garden from an old mowhay where ricks were once situated.[9] Bartholomew Gilbert, also a yeoman, or farmer, built a house on the Hill in 1796[10], and in the same year we find William Nicholls, a mason, *"lately built a dwelling house measuring outside 33ft long and 21ft wide"*.[11] In 1801 widow Ursulla Seccombe lived in a dwelling on the "Hill" built by her deceased husband Edward Seccombe.[12] He was probably a forebear of Sir Harry Secombe, the late renowned Welsh tenor, whose Cornish family migrated to Wales from the Lizard peninsula.

The families of Arthur, Willey, Richards, and the prosperous Randles appear in the seventeenth century records of Grade and Ruan Minor and the Janes and Bolithos in the early nineteenth century.

There are references in the eighteenth century to "The Great House". In 1772 Mr John Randle surrendered his lease *"of a part of the Great house in Cadgwith, formerly in the possession of his father Joseph Randle"*, to Thomas Fonnereau Esq, then the landowner of the Ruan side of Cadgwith, *"the same being three chambers and a cellar underneath the same, and the kitchen - and also that dwelling house eighteen feet in length and fourteen in breadth off from the said cellar towards the Capson House lately erected and built by the said John Randle, and also the new erected dwelling house adjoining to the last mentioned dwelling. Together with the garden lying westward of the said houses commonly called or known by the name of the four cornered garden, and also one stitch of land called the Middle Reen"* (slope or hillside).[13]

The lease was originally granted by George Mackenzie Esq., Elizabeth his wife, and significantly William Robinson whose family perhaps formerly used the

A
(present Steam Loft on right)
Western Capstan House — and Dummy's Loft
Todden Cottage
Inglewidden
The Todden
Devil's Frying Pan
CADGWITH GRADE SIDE 1841

Great House as their Cadgwith residence. It would appear to have been a complex consisting of a cellar, possibly a fish cellar, with a dwelling above it and two adjoining dwellings, known collectively as the Great House. It is shown on an undated plan of the eighteenth century roughly on the site of the present Cadgwith Hotel, which appears to be a surviving remnant of the Great House (see plan). Although heightened with brick, two rooms on the ground floor with a central passage date from the seventeenth century. The shape of the complex does not conform to that of the present Old Cellars Restaurant (Square Cellar) which must have replaced most of it. The capstan house mentioned was the Eastern Capstan House.[14] In 1799 *"R Hitchens junior"* was living in the *"house over the cellar next the Great House"*; this appears to refer to one of the dwellings above 'Square Cellar'.

Although most of the inhabitants in the 1700's appear to be tradesmen, or engaged in farming, they were probably shareholders or 'Adventurers' and actively involved in the pilchard fishery before it became solely the province of 'professional' fishermen. There were several stables, and in 1798 Alexander Tregoweth (a now lost Cornish surname) speculatively converted John Randle's old stable near the Square Garden into a blacksmith's shop, with permission to extend west as far as the 'River',[15] the stream which now divides Cadgwith. The walls were to be of stone for at least three feet, and the roof of slate. Alexander would have been engaged not only in shoeing horses and mules, and repairing agricultural implements, but in shaping iron hooks for the pressing stones of the various seine owners.

The 1841 Tithe Map and Apportionment Book for Grade shows less development on that side of Cadgwith, where much land was owned by the Hill family,

The Old Post Office, Barn Hill. c1907. (per Jocelyn Jane)

'Socoa'. 1906. (© Frank Gibson, Scilly)

and during the Victorian period by J S Davey of Bochym. When the latter acquired his property there, he erected the surviving granite gate posts to protect his rights to the road leading into the cove on that side.[16]

Much of the land west of the stream here was known collectively as Park Todden. A lease of 1836 describes the buildings then on, and adjoining the Todden itself. The lessor, Mrs I P Hill leased to Alfred Fox and William Gibbins *"All those two dwelling houses with shoemaker's shop and stable together with Plot of ground used as a garden called the Toddan in the village of Cadgwith in Grade aforesaid, in the occupation of Alice Boucher and Anthony Jane and …… Michell. Also two other dwelling houses and space in front of them in Cadgwith aforesaid, in the tenure of William Stone and Benjamin Polglase. Also that fish cellar and yard adjoining the last mentioned houses in the occupation of Richard Ivey. Also all that piece of ground lying between the said Fish cellar and the River down into the sea with the open space of ground behind the same and the bank above the same which is bounded by the road leading to the Toddan."*[17]

This complex is the present fishery cold store, previously Badgers Loft, along with the Western Capstan House and Toddan cottage. The Fox family, of Glendurgan, had for long invested in the Cornish pilchard fishing industry, and from their base at Falmouth had engaged in a profitable export business. At Cadgwith they had leased Square Cellar in 1799 as *"Messrs Fox and Partners"* and in 1856 still owned a pilchard fishery here, no doubt the cellar here discussed.[18] The names 'Hounds' Cellar and 'Badgers' Loft appear to be a reflection of the name Fox.

When building their cottages and fish cellars the inhabitants incorporated hidden cavities for the concealment of smuggled goods. Some cottages also have a door beneath the eaves of the roof at the rear, several feet above the ground with no steps leading to them. Mr Henry Jane told of a tradition that such doors were constructed as escape routes when Press Gangs descended upon the village. While the latter were delayed at the front, the fisherman descended from the elevated doorway to make his escape. The press gang, often in darkness, would either hesitate or rush into space!

Ship Cottage, on the west side of the village, has a blocked window, which features a painting of the three-masted *Socoa*, a French full-rigger wrecked near Cadgwith in 1906 with a cargo of cement, bound for San Francisco for the earthquake repairs. It was later towed into the cove. The original painting was done by Harry Arthur before he joined the navy in World War 1. He drowned when the *Queen*

Margaret was torpedoed in 1914.[19] The painting has since been altered and preserved in the conservation area as a memorial to this Cadgwith man.

In the past, the tightly knit Cornish fishing community in the cove, where many were inter- related, remained a distinct community from those beyond the confines of the little valley. In the Lizard peninsula you were once either a 'Cover' or a 'Downser' – one who lived away from the coast on the higher ground beyond. At Sennen the covers were known as 'Underhillers' and those beyond as 'Overhillers' – such was the distinction between both ways of life.   Communication was more by sea than by land.

Members of the Preventive Service, and the coastguards who followed, frequently brought new blood to the village. In 1848 it was recorded:

'The Jane Family' 1911-12. Ann and Henry Jane, grandparents, second boy from left standing, 'Buller' Arthur, Henry Jane on right front row

"The population of Cadgwith is composed principally of fishermen to whom may be added the greater part of the Preventive men belonging to the Station. Many of these last spend a considerable part of their leisure time in polishing specimens of Serpentine, and as in discharge of their duties they are obliged to perambulate the whole of the coast, they frequently fall in with the rarer and more beautiful varieties."[20]

Pilchard fishing predominated, and when catches were made, the pilchard season provided ample employment for all. The majority of males were fishermen - in 1889 there were fifty[21], and in the 1881 census reports we also find Mary Bolitho, 20 yrs., Mary Jane 16yrs., Susan Jane 17 yrs., Mary Mitchell 21yrs., and Amelia Stevens 27 yrs., – all described as *"Net Maker"*.   William Johns was the shipwright in 1851.

The village, with the added facilities of Ruan Minor churchtown, was fairly self-sufficient. In 1851 Jane Mitchell, Mary Mitchell and Archelaus Gilbert were all shopkeepers in Cadgwith; Edward and John Mitchell were shoemakers, whilst Thomas Jane was also a cordwainer, or cobbler. There were two blacksmiths at the churchtown, William Thomas and James Mundy, whose shoeing services would have been required by William Lambrick, Van proprietor[22],who ran his horse bus to and from Helston.

In 1856 John Carter was the Cadgwith tailor and by 1891 he was also the subpostmaster. Henry Jane reminisced that as a tailor he excelled in making trousers of stiff moleskin, 'Barrigan trousers' for the fishermen. Having a speech defect, before making the garment he would ask, *"What dost tha want? a fi, fap or a awl?"* – meaning "What do you want – a fly, a flap or a hole?"!

In 1881 the ladies fashion needs were provided by Dressmaker Emily Tripp, followed in 1891 by Clara Bray. For the average person to purchase clothes in a shop was almost unknown; Emily and Clara would have visited families, spending a whole day producing garments. In the same year the 'Sick Nurse' Mary Willey would have delivered their babies, and using a variety of herbal remedies, provided nursing care for all. She would also have earned a few pence for "Sitting in" at night with someone who was dying, or by "Keeping-in" with a mother and new-born baby, living in the cottage throughout the day, doing the housework and caring for mother and child until the mother had recovered sufficiently to cope.

James Nicholls was the landlord of "The Star" in 1852, since renamed the Cadgwith Hotel. He was followed in 1856 by William Bosustow[23], in 1867 by William Angove[24], and by the latters' widow Sarah, in 1871[25]. Nicholas Highman, the local police officer in 1861 would have dealt with any rowdiness there.

For centuries the population of Ruan Minor had taken their corn to be ground to the surviving manor mill at Poltesco, situated in its quiet and remote valley. Those who lived on Grade Side at Cadgwith, probably used Ledra, or Luddra mill, which was powered by the stream which descends to the cove. (Ledra is Cornish for a slope). It was for long used by the prosperous Randle family who were quite influential at Cadgwith throughout the eighteenth and nineteenth centuries. John Randle was involved in the development of the fishing industry here in 1780, and was joined by James in renting 'Square Cellar' and its capstan house. John was also an Adventurer or shareholder in the fishery at Church Cove, Landewednack in 1782,[26] and in 1856 'Randle and Co. Pilchard Fishery' was listed at Cadgwith.[27] Thomas Randle was the miller at Ledra Mill in 1841, where he and Nicholas Randle leased both the tenement and fields at St. Ruan; at the same time Joseph farmed at Engewidden (today 'Inglewidden'), adjoining the Devils Frying Pan.[28]

Much of their wealth is said to have derived from their smuggling activities with the famous smuggler Harry Carter, the 'King of Prussia', to whom they were related by marriage. Robert Randle used his mill at Ledra as a distribution centre for contraband landed at Cadgwith.[29] In 1871 Richard Carter, born in 1797 was the miller there.

The Cox family were also fairly prosperous. Henry Cox, a good amateur photographer, had come from Lincolnshire and was manager of the serpentine works at Poltesco in 1856.[30] By 1871, when he was sixty, his son, Henry Jnr., born in London, succeeded him at Poltesco, whilst his father became the manager of the Cadgwith Seining Co. and lived with his family at Poltesco House, with two servants and a nurse.

The latter cared for the four children of his daughter, Jeanette Raven.[31] Henry Jane recalled that a Miss Raven lived in the cottage situated above the cove just below Man-o-War path in the 1890's. There is a small cave on that side of Fishing cove, which is known as 'Miss Raven's Ugoo' (Ugoo or Ogo is Cornish for cave) probably named after some incident which occurred there.

James Nicholls, born locally, and who died in 1869 at Cadgwith, was an enterprising person who in 1851 was a farmer, and also landlord of The Star.[32] In his last will and testament he bequeathed to his son "*All my parts, or shares, and interest of in, or to all seins, boats and in fishing tools, tackle and materials at Cadgwith and elsewhere..... and to my coalyard and premises in, or near to Cadgwith.*"[33]

'The Post', (Author)

His son Joseph, or 'Cap'n Joe' who inherited the coal yard lived on 'Ruan Side' in 1891, as farmer and coal merchant. The 1841 the map of Ruan Minor shows a large area in the centre of the village known as The Square from its shape. It has since been much built upon, and is fronted by 'Square Cellar' which takes its name from the site. There was once a cobbled yard here where coal was stored for distribution in the locality. In the eighteenth century it was taken to the Lizard lighthouse for its coal fired beacons which were lit by oil in 1813.[34]

Coastal schooners called at Cadgwith; in 1846 the *Venus* of Bideford, discharged part of her cargo of coal on the beach at Fishing Cove, and then lay off shore. A gale blew up, and cries for help were heard by the Cadgwith fishermen, who took off her crew and later towed the vessel into sea-room.[35]

The Chapel of St. Mary, (Author)

Coastal schooner in
Fishing Cove 1907.
(Cornwall Centre)

At the turn of the twentieth century as much as 100 tons of coal were still being landed at Fishing Cove. The arrival of the schooner was always an event in the village. Henry Jane recalled,

"One of the schooners was the Fanny, sailed by a Captain Lammy. It tied up to the 'pawst', which was also used by the lifeboat. ('Pawst' or 'post', the large cylindrical granite bollard still to be seen.)   Cap'n Joe Nicholls owned the coal yard. He lived in a house on Man-o-War path. Being a heavy smoker he was always sending boys to the shop for 'Westward Ho' tobacco, so we made up the following rhyme:
'Westward Ho!
And a rumble Oh!
An ounce of baccy
For Capn Joe!'"

Although the beauty of Cadgwith was somewhat marred in the Victorian period by the oppressive odour of fish and fish-bait from its cellars, visitors and artists were not deterred. In 1878 Mr T Williams of the Cadgwith Hotel was entertaining people of rank,[36] and in 1889 there were two lodging houses.

The religious needs of the population had for long been provided by the churches of Grade and Ruan Minor, and by local chapels, but in 1895 Charles H Thursby built the small Catholic chapel of the Holy Cross on the Grade side of Cadgwith near his dwelling. It is now Anglican. The name reflects that of Grade parish, which in 1261 was called 'St.Cross'. It would appear that at some time prior to that date, Sir William Wallysborough of Cornwall returned from a pilgrimage with a fragment of the True Cross, stolen from the Holy Sepulchre. His vessel was wrecked on the shores of Grade, and as he vowed to give a piece of this relic to the church of the parish where he might safely land, he gave it to the church there, where in 1553, the 'Holy Cross' was kept in a silver box.[37]

Kelly's Directory of 1897 describes the Cadgwith chapel as *"a small building of wood"* and states that *"divine service is held regularly"*. It was dedicated on the 5th February 1898 to St Mary, by the Bishop of Truro.[38] Today it is of galvanised iron and wood, with a miniature steeple and a bell above the west porch. In its simplicity, the interior is not unlike a small wayside chapel of Greece.

Near the path, below the church is an overgrown well which provided water for much of the village. It once had a wooden door and was white washed inside. The path beyond the church ends at 'Cripples Corner', where it enters the large car park adjoining 'Donkey Field'.[39]

"MEAT, MONEY . . ."

Those who dwelt at Cadgwith in the 1700s, would have known the quay there, which is, seemingly, depicted in the Lanydrock Atlas of 1696; it must have extended across much of the entrance to 'Fishing Cove', and probably incorporated the little peninsula known as the 'Todden', as a means of approach. The latter, meaning a grassy area, divides the cove into 'Cadgwith Cove' or 'Fishing Cove', to the east, and 'Little Cove' to the west. We can surmise that sections of the quay were probably shaped out of the Todden itself, and the remainder built with blocks of stone. In 1799 C Polkinhorn wrote to Sir Christopher Hawkins' Steward, Mr G H Chilcott:

"Sir, you was speaking of rebuilding the Quay at Cadgwith. If you thought anything of it, I would advise you to get the large stones that was formerly in the same, but now is in the river, and the beach washed off from them, taken up, as it will be done for little expense before the beach is settled on them again." [1.]

The Quay had obviously been washed away, and its stone blocks had lain, covered with sand, until they were exposed at that period. Such a quay would have been accessible both from the shore, and from the Todden. Although it was, apparently, never rebuilt, the pilchard seining industry was greatly improved both here and at Church Cove, Landewednack, by the landowners, the Hawkins of Trewithen, who had purchased the Ruan Minor side of the cove in 1780.[2]

The quay would have provided shelter for numerous small fishing boats which probably resembled the luggers of Mounts Bay in use in 1790; these had a 25ft keel with a strong curve in the stern. The accommodation for the crew was meagre, *"a short deck at the bow, about eight or ten feet long, was all the covering afforded"*[3]. Their cooking facility was a "Maenollas" or "Mynolla" (Cornish *maen* = stone, *olas* = a hearth), a piece of hollowed-out granite placed in the open part of the boat, on which a fire was lit, *"while the crew, wrapped in their capes, a large coarse covering enveloping the head and body in one garment, sought their repose beneath a sail, or in any sheltered nook on the weather quarter that could be obtained."* [4]

However, it was, pilchard seining which predominated at Cadgwith, involving a different type of vessel. The seine boat, which carried the huge seine net was usually about 33ft long with a 12ft beam, both large and heavy. It was manned by six or eight rowers, with a helmsman using an oar at the rear to steer it.[5] The 'Follower' was a boat of similar design to the seine boat and carried the 'stop-seine', which was used to close the gap in the seine net. The 'tuck-net' was carried by a smaller boat. At Cadgwith in 1782, seven men manned each seine boat and four the 'Follower'.[6]

Pilchard seining, with a vast market available in Italy and the Adriatic Sea,

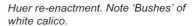
Huer re-enactment. Note 'Bushes' of white calico.

was, with mining, a major Cornish industry. Nearly every small cove in the Lizard and the Land's End peninsulas had a small seining company. Some comprised of miners and farmers, but here at the Lizard, fishing was a full time occupation for many, with long established fish cellars at Cadgwith, Carleon (Poltesco) and Church Cove. From August to November or December, large shoals of pilchard appeared almost annually off the Cornish coast turning the sea into a purple hue as they passed along.

It was the 'balker' or 'huer' who waited on the cliffs for their appearance in order to signal to the seine boats lying off-shore. He was, with the master seiner, the highest paid. The movement of the water, the activity of the gulls and the diving of gannets, all alerted him to the presence of a shoal, and he could often even tell which fish were present by their actions. If porpoises or fish were sighted close to shore it was a sure sign of an impending gale.[7]. He also decided when the seine boats should be positioned off shore and manned in readiness.[8].

The Cadgwith huer would have had a good vantage point from the cliff top near the old Coastguard Watchhouse, and at Polbarrow where the seine-boats were often kept afloat in readiness. There, iron rings were driven into the rocks to secure the seine in position when full of fish if 'tucking' was delayed.   There too are traces of a small hut once used by the seiners.

Two fields above the Watchhouse are called 'Beacon Field' and 'Beacon Croft' on the Tithe Apportionment of 1841. Research by this writer has shown that 'Beacon', when situated above a fishing cove, can be a corruption of 'Bawken' referring to a 'Bawken House' or 'Balking-house';[9] this was either a temporary shelter or a stone built hut where the huer stored his implements. The name derives from the Cornish '*bawk*', to shout, reflecting the shouts of the huer which accompanied his simple signals.[10] These were given in most coves by using a gorse bush, dipped in whitewash and held in either hand. The signals indicated the position and movements of the pilchards to the men in the boats. At a later date these were replaced by 'bushes' of white calico, resembling balloons on sticks. A long megaphone of tin, the 'Huer's

Horn', was also used to shout directions. The word 'Balk' is also found at Church Cove nearby, and at other places along the Cornish coast.

However, it is more likely that 'Beacon Field' was the site of the early warning beacon of Ruan Minor, kept in readiness as an alert, from the reign of Henry VIII until the wars with France. In 1848 a mound of loose stones, enclosed by others fixed in the ground in the form of a circle stood near the Flagstaff, presumably the Watchhouse, and not 'Signal staff'. There were similar mounds at the Rill, and Trewavas Head – all

21

believed to be beacon platforms.[11].

When the pilchards were sighted, the alerting cry, in Cornish, of 'Hevva' was normally used, which derived from the old Cornish '*hedfa*', meaning 'swarming' or 'flocking'[12]. At Cadgwith the cry was usually 'Hubba' – a corruption of 'Hevva'; at Sennen Cove it was 'Owé', and at St Just 'Ové'[13]. The cry would be taken up in the cove, where all and sundry rushed to prepare for the catch. Such a scene at 'Cadgwith' was described in 1885:

"It is really exciting to hear the pilchard cry for the first time, and when the visitors are new to this sound, they rise and leave their dinner or amusements and rush en masse to see what is happening. For when a shoal has come within reach, every man who dwells in the village, whatever he may be engaged in doing, is called by a strange, terrible cry to come and help in the take! And he comes generally at a gallop, and breathless. The boats are always ready in the bay".[14.]

Karen Tangye with Gurry, Square Cellar, 1972 (Author)

The scene continues with a further description in 1893:

"We saw to the westward a long reddish line advancing slowly, towards the Lizard, and behind it a huge flock of sea-birds, one of which, now and again, darted down into the agitated water.
The huers were now armed with bushes by which they directed the movements of some half a dozen large rowing boats, which they had put forth with seines, and in an hour a great part of the shoal was enclosed. Through the whole of the summer night and far into the next day, every available person was employed in removing the fish to smaller nets, and thence to boats which conveyed them to the shore; barrows and baskets finally carrying them to the curing cellars where the female population arranged them in tiers and salted them" all amidst *"a babel of voices, jesting and quarrelling"*[15].

The story was told at Cadgwith, in 1897, of a veteran huer who was considered to be a source of bad luck after several missed catches. A conference was held by the superstitious seiners who decided to give him one more chance, and if not successful, another huer was to be appointed. The old huer passed a restless night, and rose early in the morning telling his wife, "There is fish about!" *"The seine was shot and a substantial sum went to each man – and honours for the old huer!"*[16].

To explain the shooting of the seine and the curing process in more detail: –

Guided by the huer, two seine boats, which usually lay stern to stern, started off in opposite directions to make a wide circle about the purple stain, sowing their brown nets upon the green water, marked at the top by their attached corks and floats and weighted with lead at the bottom. The 'Follower', a smaller boat with two or three men, then joined up the nets using a 'stop-net', beating the water with oars to prevent the fish from darting away. The seine net was sometimes left a day or so before tucking commenced.

A smaller boat, bearing the 'tuck net', passed over the seine net, and, with others, drove the fish into one corner of the huge 'paddock' created by again beating the water with oars. The tuck net was then let down surrounding them, its foot ropes enabling it to be drawn together like a bag. The upper edge of the net was then made fast to the seine boats while the shouting men in the tuck-boat hauled in the slack until the mass of silver pilchards came to the surface. As the fish were poured into the boats from baskets, the water drained through the bulkheads and a boy also baled it out. Each boat usually held from seven to nine hogsheads of pilchards and were not considered to be full until nearly awash, and got away with difficulty to be replaced by others.[17.]

Although in most cases the fish were taken to Mevagissey, Falmouth, Porthleven, or Newlyn, to be bought and cured by larger concerns, much was cured in the various fish cellars at Cadgwith, to which they were carried by men and boys using a 'gurry', a large wooden box with handles fore and aft, and by horse and cart.

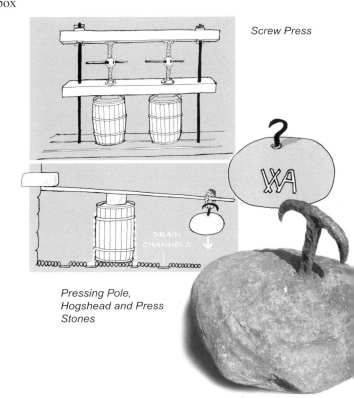

Screw Press

In the several cellars, the pilchards were placed in 'bulk' by women and girls known as 'bulkers' – built up to a rectangular mass about five feet high with alternate layers of fish and salt, the latter scooped up with wooden shovels by boys: *"They are all hard at work and are quite silent; the "Who wants fish here?" "Salt here?" of the carriers is all that is heard. They are too much in earnest to talk."*[18.]

Pressing Pole, Hogshead and Press Stones

All in contrast to the 'babel' observed on the other occasion, but all dwelling on the old saying,

"Meat, money and light – All in one night"[19.]

Another reporter observed such a scene: *"A cellar full of pilchards is a strange sight. You scarcely see the salt in which they are bedded, or the tails of alternate layers; you only notice the grim looking heads, open- mouthed, rising row upon row, almost to the roof, the highest layer being topped with heavily weighted boards."*[20.].

After four or five weeks the salt had been absorbed and the bulk was broken, the pilchards washed and placed neatly into casks, or hogsheads, each containing about 2900 – 4000 summer pilchards or 2300 – 2900 winter pilchards, and weighing 476 lbs gross.[21] These were then placed in rows fronting the cellar walls, in which were square recesses, which personal observation shows were normally about 2ft apart and 3ft 7ins above floor level.[22] Into these were slotted pressing-poles or press-poles, squared timbers which projected over a block of wood laid on the wooden lid of the hogshead or 'buckler'. From the end of each pole a heavy pressing-stone was suspended from a strop of rope by an iron hook set firmly in a central sinking of lead. The considerable weight of the pressing-stone pressed the pole down on the over-filled hogshead forcing the oil and brine from between the loose staves. Fresh pilchards were added as the others were compressed.

One pressing-stone survives at Cadgwith, but several were found during the conversion of Badger's Loft to a cold store in 1998; in West Cornwall round and oval granite beach boulders were used, and at Harlyn Bay rectangular blocks of local stone. The shape of the hook varied. At St Ives, Mr Brian Stevens found several pressing-stones with the seine owner's initials carved on them.

Most hogsheads at Cadgwith and Church cove were pressed by wedging the pressing-pole beneath a stone projection along the cellar wall. Such examples, once known as a 'run'[23] survive at Cadgwith on the interior and exterior west wall of Square Cellar; those outside were once sheltered by a lean-to roof, but are now enclosed by a dwelling. In some coves, a long wooden beam, supported by upright irons driven through it, ran the whole length of the cellar, beneath which pressing poles were wedged. Such a beam survives in 'Big Cellar' at Penberth Cove, Land's End. Screw-presses were normally smaller, and following their introduction in the 1870's sometimes supplanted the older method of using pressing-poles. No tradition of screw-presses survives at Cadgwith, although 'steeping vats' of brine were used there, following their introduction at Mevagissey in 1876,[24] instead of placing them in bulk. Such vats replaced barrels of brine and produced bright, salted pilchards attractive for the Mediterranean market. The pilchards once washed and pressed, were known as 'fermades' or 'fairmaids', which derived from the Spanish '*fumados*', in reference to the earlier process of partly smoking them before export.

The pressing took seven days, forcing the train-oil (Dutch *traan* – fish oil)[25] from between the loose staves of the hogshead to drain along narrow channels between the cobbled floors, or along a planked surface, into a rectangular or circular 'train-pit', commonly known as a 'drug-pit' (*dreg*), the latter sometimes fitted with a barrel. Unlike such large fishing communities as St Ives and Newlyn, there was probably not sufficient oil to be sent to Bristol and London to be used for lighting, tanning and as cod-liver oil, but it provided lighting for the cottages of Cadgwith and the surrounding area.

The Master Seiner and the Huer were the highest paid in any seining company, along with the Fish Curer who supervised the cellars. In 1782 William Jago of Lostwithiel was offered such a latter position at nearby Church Cove, at an annual salary of six shillings per week. He was also paid *"1s per Hogshead for Tunning the Oil"*; in the *"salt employ to be allowed 1s 6d per day expenses"*.[26] Salt was imported, or smuggled, from France and stored within the Salt House of each cellar.[27] He also had to purchase a sixteenth share in the company. No doubt the same conditions applied at Cadgwith.

SEINES AND SEINERS

Reports of the fishing industry at Cadgwith occasionally appeared in the Cornish press. In 1811 the seine there took 100 hogsheads of pilchards,[1] and although 600 hogsheads were reported taken in October1823,[2] the pilchards had failed to appear in viable numbers off the Cornish coast from 1816 to that year. It was perhaps this fact which brought about the auction of two seines at the Cadgwith house of Samuel Johnson in 1825:

"Cadgwith Sean – consisting of two stop and one tuck seans with boats and materials complete. Also the Carclew Sean lying at Cadgwith, two stops and one tuck Seans with boats and materials complete. Well situated, having the command of Kennick Bay. For details to William Blake & Co. of St. Mawes, and for viewing to George Boulden, Cadgwith."[3]

In 1867 C.H.T. Hawkins, the landowner, wrote to the Cadgwith Seine (fishery) Co. saying that the rent of the cellars was very low, and accused them of *"carrying on the Fishery with indifference and little energy"*. This was denied, and it was stated that they *"had secured more fish in our seines than any other party in the Bay for the last twenty years"*, involving both energy and expense. Concerning the rent, it was stated that this was low when no fish were caught *"but 1s per hogshead is paid (to the leaseholder) for fish cured at Cadgwith"*.[4]

The Cadgwith Seine Co. were again experiencing problems in May 1875 when G.C. Fox and Co., the owners, settled with the leaseholder the sum of £15 for the annual rent of their cellars, and £5 in money due for 100 hogsheads, and added in their correspondence, *"Deciding that a considerable outlay was required to put the concern in an efficient state, the company decided in selling the seines and other effects and winding up their affairs"*.[5] The 'Alfred Seines' were, apparently bought by Mr.Henry Cox of Cadgwith, who was described in the 1881 census as 'Sean Owner'.

Pilchard seine fishing flourished at Cadgwith between 1870 and 1890. In November 1884 one catch, referred to as a 'Hobble', realised £1400, with £700 going to the fishermen. One school was lost, as the sea was too rough to launch the boats; the following day several seines were out, one was shot but missed, a second seine enclosed a large shoal, but rough conditions swept the net corks under, allowing the fish to escape. However, *"Mr. Cox was fortunate. His seines enclosed about 400 hogsheads of very fine pilchards, and succeeded in tucking the whole"*. A portion was landed to be cured at Cadgwith, the remainder being taken to Newlyn and sold by auction, realising the unprecedented price of 9s 1d per basket, when £3 3s per hogshead was formerly considered good value for the fish when cured and sold.[6]

In October 1885 all was excitement and hurry as large shoals passed the Lizard. The Lizard Fishing Co. of Church Cove, shot three seines, securing 400 hogsheads of fish in two, but lost a third fine shoal through a defective net. Messrs Cox and Co. of Cadgwith, also enclosed a good shoal, and because of stormy westerly winds preventing the boats from rounding the Lizard, they were taken ashore at Cadgwith for curing *"giving ample employment for all the women, boys and girls in the district. This means a considerable sum of money circulated in the district in addition to the men's shares. The boats have a fifth of all the fish for carrying to Newlyn, and the curing wages will be spent at the Lizard instead of at Newlyn. Probably when the railway is extended to the Lizard all pilchards caught on this coast will be cured there. The obstacle now is the enormous expense of so long a cartage to the port of shipment. The Lizard beaches are too hazardous in the winter for vessels to fetch them."*[7]

The railway was never constructed, and so catches at Cadgwith continued to be taken by Newlyn vessels to that port, and by others to Falmouth and Mevagissey, where, once prepared, they were packed into hogsheads and shipped to Italy and the Adriatic for consumption, particularly during Lent.[8]

At the end of the summer mackerel season in June some Cadgwith vessels

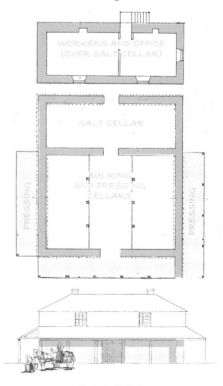

ROAD END ELEVATION

Above:- Plan of Fish Cellar, Church Cove, Landewednack, 1837. (After Plan Cornwall Record Office)
Left:- The Fish Cellar and Round Capstan House. Old Lifeboat House in foreground.

27

Cadgwith fishermen and coast guards. C1900. Anthony Jane (rt with white coat) Henry Jane 4th left front, black jersey (per Jocelyn Jane)

joined others from Mount's Bay, Penzance, for the Irish fishing grounds for herring and pilchards. Some vessels continued on to Aberdeen in July, with most returning by the first week in August for the Cornish pilchard season.[9]

Although St. Ives vessels had for long sailed to the rich Irish fishing grounds, it was Captain Charles Kelynack of Newlyn, who first introduced the source to the Mount's Bay and Lizard fishermen, in 1820-21. His father, Mr Philip Kelynack, protected the Rev. John Wesley from a hostile crowd at Newlyn in 1747[10]. Between the June and August of 1836 and 1837, 136 herring boats from Mount's Bay were joined by one from Sennen and 25 from St. Ives, for Ireland to earn £10,000, after paying all costs.[11]

Amongst those Cadgwith fishermen who made the long voyage, in the 1880's, was the late "Buller" Arthur's grandfather, Henry Jane, who was accompanied by his wife Ann. Whilst in Ireland *they saw a deposit of fish scales, several feet thick*.[12] They had probably sailed with a company formed by John Cox of Cadgwith, named in the 1881 census as living in the 'Ruan Side' of the village, and as *Manager, Fishing Co. Born London*. Cox, wishing to revive the pilchard fishing industry at Baltimore, built fish cellars there in 1876, and staffed it with Cornishmen in 1877. When digging the foundations for a cellar, *the workmen came upon a deposit of pilchard scales several feet thick".*[13]

From the 1870's the pilchard industry declined and, in October 1893, although it made a large catch, much of it was used for manuring the ground because of an unremunerative market.[14] By 1896, 500 lobsters and 1000 crabs, besides crayfish, were sold to merchants weekly.[15]

Details of this, and other aspects, were given in a government report at that time. Although there were still five pilchard seines active, other boats were used for crabbing and long line, *"and are open boats 16ft – 18ft long. Boat building none. Usually made at Falmouth. Trawls none. Trammels average 4 to a boat. Pots 60-70 per boat. Crabs stored and are sent to Falmouth, 12-14 landed daily. Crabs large and good – Cocks 1s 3d. Hens 3d. Bait-Ray and Skate, but any trammed fish. Bought off long-liners from Falmouth, who call here. Lobsters good – Cocks 1s 6d, Hens 1s. Cray fish very fair numbers – same price as lobsters.*

Crabbing – coast difficult. Except by old men, very little is done within 1 mile of shore except at beginning of season, Feb' and March when weather does not permit them going out farther.

Fishing Ground – in semi-circular line, Blackhead to Rill, 5 miles deep. The crabbers put 6 crab pots to a string, called, 'Bar Bells'. Want of suitable harbour accommodation prevents the men from employing larger boats".[16]

Fishing for lobster and crab became more important as pilchards diminished. The pots were made from willows, which were grown at most fishing coves in 'Withy Gardens'. The crab pot stand on which they were constructed consists of a circular disc, with 40 holes arranged in two rows for making two sizes of pot, surmounting a wooden post, called a 'Pot stand'

Fieldwork has shown that two or three men often worked together. At Penberth, near the Land's End, one specialised in sharpening the withies, one made the top, the other the bottom. Cadgwith men worked the withies anti-clockwise, whereas Mullion men worked clock-wise. At Cadgwith the base of the pot is called the 'chim' the centre of the base the 'navel', and the entrance the 'funnel' or 'mouth'. Withies were bent using a 'knee-stool', two pieces of wood set close together. When making a pot, one started with the 'standards', then the 'ribs', one on each side, and for extra space at the bottom – a 'pitcher'. Local black withies were used for the 'ribs'

Henry Jane with Pot-Stand 1973
(Author)

and 'chim', whilst superior Somerset withies were used for the 'funnel'. When withies were trimmed, turned and pointed, a man could make eight pots in a day, with an expected 'life' of from three to four months.

A weighting stone was secured to the base of the pot with rope passed through the 'chim' with the aid of a 'stoning-iron', a piece of metal 2 – 3 feet long with an eye at the extremity. A loop was made when it was threaded. Bait was placed inside on a 'preen', a short, sharpened forked stick.[17]

In 1897 the Cadgwith Seining Co. distributed share money following the catch of 150 hogsheads of pilchards. About fifty men received £2 16s upwards, and 12s per share was paid on 100 shares, mostly held by fishermen.[18]

Lady Fish Hawker.
C1906.
Female fish
'Jousters' carried
fish in a basket on
their back.

Although the pilchard fishing era was drawing to a close, vast catches were made in the early nineteen hundreds. When the 'Cadgwith Covers Fishing Co.' shot their seine at Polbarrow in September 1901, they enclosed 200,000 pilchards which were bought at 8s 6d per 1000 by Mevagissey buyers and taken by boats to Newlyn.[19]

1904 proved to be a highly successful season. That November the Covers seine enclosed a large shoal on the Tuesday, but being stormy they left them in the seine net until the Thursday; whilst tucking them the cry of 'Hevva' made them proceed to their Lizard stem where they secured another shoal, and yet others were tucked at Polbarrow on the Saturday. The whole provided £1000 which was divided between the seiners and shareholders. As most of the latter were seiners the money provided for them throughout the winter;[20] it was also the custom at the end of the season for the Cadgwith men to have half the fish caught and no pay. The wives also benefited when the manager of the Covers Company gave two guineas *"to be equally divided among the Cadgwith fisherwomen who so willingly responded when called upon to help in launching the seine boats in a time of Hevva"*.[21] The Badgers Company, however, had failed to catch any fish.

In the autumn of 1908 huge shoals of pilchards passed between the Lizard and Falmouth. That September the Badgers secured a shoal at Cadgwith Cove, whilst the Covers secured two shoals at Polbarrow. The interest and excitement created was reported to have been intense , and created quite a spectacle for visitors.[22] As a boy, Richard 'Buller' Arthur (1901-1981) recalled six seine boats at the cove before 1914, and he was also present when the seine was shot at Polbarrow on this occasion, *"I remember the fish being tucked, but this was the last seine to be shot at Polbarrow. By the 1920's the pilchard fishery had ended. At that time the familiar purple hue seen on the water of the cove appeared to be a shoal of pilchards; the seine was shot, only to discover the fish were sardines!"*

The totals of the vast catches made in 1904 and 1908 were recorded on a beam in the loft above the Winch House: *"Fish caught 1904. Oct 18th, 303,000 at 12s and 8s per Thou'. Nov 8th, 10th and 11th, 1,798,000 at 12/3d, 12/-, 10/- and 8/6 per thousand. 1908 September 4th 786,000. Sept 15th 227,000, 22nd 71,000. 24th, 25th 1,347,000"*

Henry Jane at Old Barkhouse in the Square, also used for boat-building. Note drying pole for nets (Author)

The long history of the pilchard fishery at Cadgwith had finally, apparently ceased. For some unknown reason the pilchard ceased to appear in great numbers off the Cornish coast. However, during the 1930s it was possible to buy pilchards locally from fish hawkers, who drove carts frantically from village to village with their familiar cry of "Pilchay! Pilchay!". Most Cornish families salted a winters supply in a tall 'bussa', a large earthenware container. Bushes of bay leaf survive today in most communities, once used with vinegar and spices to marinate the pilchards. Yet there are hopes at Cadgwith of a revival, as Cadgwith fisherman Martin Ellis obtained a good living catching pilchards, which have again appeared off the coast.

Other forms of fishing have continued to the present time, but it has always been a dangerous occupation, and many Cadgwith fishermen have been drowned over a long period. In 1842, John and Michael Taylor were both drowned at Cadgwith when a heavy sea swamped their boat.[23]

In 1874 four men put off in a boat to bring ashore withies, brought by a fishing smack from the East coast, for making lobster pots. Their boat capsized, three being saved by clinging to bundles of withies, but Alec Cliff drowned.[24]

In more recent times the village was cast into gloom following the drowning of Tony Culmer and Peter Williams, both lost at sea in March 1994. A plaque to their memory can be seen on the Winch-house.

Fishing vessels needed frequent repairs and there was often the need of a new small boat. A building which survives in the 'Square' was used for boat building, perhaps by William Johns, described in 1851 as *'Shipwright'*, and subsequently as *'Ships Carpenter'*.[25] No doubt he made small vessels at Cadgwith. Edward Rutter, described in 1910 as *'Fisherman, Coxswain of Lifeboat, Sub Postmaster'*, succeeded him, and constructed 24 feet crab-boats in the same building, where a wall had to be taken down to remove vessels when completed! Alfred Willey followed, building small boats below 16 feet in length, but after the 1939-1945 war he made one of 20 feet.[26]

CADGWITH WHALERS

Whales, turtles and sharks have for long strayed into Cornish waters, the whales creating great excitement within fishing communities. In the summer of 1843, a large whale, which had been seen off the Lizard and Porthleven for several weeks, appeared off Cadgwith, creating considerable damage to crab-pots. Seven men, in one of the large seine-boats, attacked the creature with a harpoon, without success. In a second attempt the harpoon embedded itself into its side, whereupon it immediately dived and headed out to sea, towing the boat after it at the rate of at least six miles an hour.

Realising it was a hopeless task, the Cadgwith 'Moby Dicks', reluctantly released the rope. The whale was last seen delightedly throwing its huge tail at least eight feet out of the water to a considerable height.[1]

There was a similar episode at Cadgwith in March 1863, when the community awoke to find a large whale within the cove. Two fishermen, who had possibly taken part in the earlier incident, hurriedly constructed a harpoon from a stout pole and a piece of sharpened iron, and set off in a small boat, and plunging the weapon into the huge creature.

The wounded whale immediately headed off in the direction of Falmouth, towing the boat behind it! It was not until midday, when the Eddystone lighthouse, off Plymouth, came into view, that the two Cadgwith men decided it was time to abandon their prize. Cutting it loose, they proceeded on the long row back to Cadgwith where they arrived the following day in an exhausted condition. There they were greeted by

Leather Back Turtle. Fishing Cove 1971

the whole village with joking and bantering.[2]

As if in defiance of its persecutors, the whale shortly returned again to the waters of the Lizard with the large 'harpoon' still firmly embedded in its body. This became entangled in the lines and moorings of crabbing gear owned by fishermen of the Lizard Fishery at Church Cove, which it *"towed away behind it in a long trail"*. The angry fishermen, unable to obtain their livelihood, threatened to bring an action against the Cadgwith 'whalers' for leaving the pole in the back of the creature![3]

In August, the same year, yet another whale entered the cove at Cadgwith only to be stranded, and to die on the rocks. It was taken by the fishermen and towed to Falmouth by a steamer sent by Mr Fox, where its huge bulk, seventy-four feet long and twenty-four feet in circumference, was for some time placed on the docks gridiron for public viewing.

Coinciding, as it did, with the opening of the Falmouth railway, it was seen by thousands, *"but the nauseous smell at length caused it to be removed to the outer end of the breakwater, and it has since been cut up"*.[4]

A swordfish, the natural enemy of the whale, about eleven feet long, had been reported by huers at St Ives bay at this time, and its presence was said to account for the whale stranded at Cadgwith.[5] The 'swords' of the swordfish once hung in Square Cellar (1972), along with an iron spearhead reputed to have been used for shark fishing; its wide, hinged barbs would extend by a pull on the shaft once the shark had been speared.

CELLARS, LOFTS AND CAPSTANS

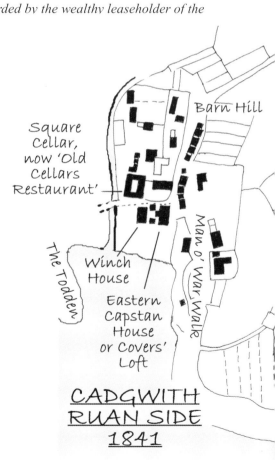

It is difficult to accurately date the numerous cellars and lofts at Cadgwith, and equally difficult to identify the numerous owners and occupiers of the past. Fortunately, both the late Henry Jane and Richard 'Buller' Arthur retained traditional memories which allow us to name certain buildings as they were known at the turn of the last century.

The most important asset of any cove was its capstan, normally provided by the leaseholder of the cove, and from which he obtained either a fee or a tithe in fish. An observer commented on this subject in 1873:

"Fishermens' seines are not well regarded by the wealthy leaseholder of the cove and foreshore, and the leaseholder has legal powers and rights which it would be idle to blame him for exercising.

The cots are his, and the capstan is his, so he can put on the screw when he wants to have his own way, and can threaten evictions, the withdrawal of the right to the capstan, and to the landing place, if the men will not go on his seine but choose either a united one, or independent. On the whole, the Cornish fisherman of the smaller coves has not much to boast of beside his courage and good heart, and a sturdy independence and honesty specially noticeable."[1]

The fishermen of Cadgwith were fortunate in that they appear to have enjoyed a good relationship with their main leaseholder, the Hawkins family of Trewithen, and their descendants.

In 1782 the Hawkins family had invested heavily in the development of fisheries both at Cadgwith and Church Cove, Landewednack. At that time they stated that the usual way of paying and renting the fish cellars at each cove was to pay 1s per hogshead of all fish cured, or at a fixed rent, according to the landlord's wishes.

For the use of the capstan *"each seyner pays 1s yearly, and the Craft or Seyne Adventurer pays as much as all the men."* At Cadgwith each boat paid 5s a year to the capstan *"and each seyner pays 1s a year for the use of the capstan rope besides the 5s paid for the boat. Strangers' boats, belonging to ships, pay 3d for drawing up boats."*[2]

Today fishing vessels are hauled up the beach by an electric winch, assisted by the traditional method of placing 'timbers', short lengths of rounded wood, in front of the vessel to assist its progress. We will never know when a capstan was first placed in the cove, but one of the earliest examples was situated in the building known as 'Bay View', but formerly as *'Little Capstan House', 'Eastern Capstan Loft',* or *'Covers' Loft'* which was built before 1772.

Now a dwelling, it was ideally situated in the eastern corner of Fishing Cove, in an elevated position away from high seas. It is fronted by a wide slipway up which the heavy seine boats were hauled by several men straining to turn the arms of the great wooden capstan. An adjoining terrace provided an area for boats in winter, and a drying area for nets. Fish appear to have been pressed in the lower section of the capstan-house, as a 'dreg pit', filled with French wine bottles, was found there many years ago. An old jib, once used for lifting purposes at the foot of the slipway, has for long been destroyed.[3]

In the will of John Randle of Grade, dated 8th September 1781, he left to James his son, *"The house and garden he now lives in at Cadgwith"*, and also to James and his brother Edward, as tenants in common, *"all my Capstand at Cadgwith in the parish of Ruan Minor, with Ropes and materials thereto belonging."*

A plan of the property shows it to be the 'Eastern Capstan House' we see today. James added a room on the west side in his garden, *"lately built in 1784, a new room and chamber over"*.[4] Nicholas Randle occupied it in 1841, when it was known as 'Little Capstan House'.[5] In the early years of the twentieth century it was used by a seining company called the 'Covers' and was known as 'Covers Loft'.[6]

Great Capstan House, Boat House or Winch House - To the west of the Eastern capstan lies the present 'Winch house' or 'Boat House'. It appears to have been built in 1782 to house a capstan. There was probably a large wooden example with four arms on the site prior to its construction.

By building Capstand (sic) house at Cadgwith	£53.5.7.	
By clearing the plot for building as per contract	£5.10.0.	
By bill for taking down the walls of the Capstand,		
and ridding the foundation under the inspection		
of John Randle.	£4.4.0	£62.19.7[7]

So the capstan, possibly with its circular walled enclosure, similar to one

Top Left:- Square Cellar with'The Stick' (Bench)
Inset:- 'JFS 1908'. John F Stephens
Centre:- 'Fishing Cove' Ruan Side

Seine Boats

Top right:- Great Capstan House winch (now located outsi
Building is now calld 'Winch House'. (Author 1972).
Bottom left:- 10 man winch outside Winch-House.
Bottom right:- Capstan, 'Eastern Capstan House'. 1885

surviving at Penberth Cove, was removed to make room for the present Winch-House, where a capstan was placed to haul up the boats associated with 'Square Cellar', which lies behind it. Traces of this capstan remained in the walls of the upper section in 1972, and it was probably this same building, earlier thatched, which was later leased;

"Jan 14th 1802, conditions of a Survey held this 14th day of January 1802 at the house of John Hall in Ruan Minor Churchtown, by G H Chilcott on the behalf of Sir Christopher Hawkins, Baronet, for selling a lease for three lives of All That Capstan House in the village of Cadgwith late in possession of Messrs fox and partners, but now of John Randle, being about 41 feet long and 23 feet wide with a loft over the same.... To be reserved the liberty of the free use of the said capstan to all the tenants of the said Sir C Hawkins, and tenants and occupiers of cellars on payment of usual fee.

The purchaser is also covenanted to contribute one half towards building the quay at Cadgwith, and after it is built to be kept in repair - the other half by purchasers of the Fish Cellars "[8]

This was also, obviously, an attempt to finance the rebuilding of the quay which had been destroyed in the previous century.

In 1841 it was known as 'Great Capstan House' when it was occupied by Nicholas Randle.[9] The capstan of 1782 was later replaced by a winch, which in 1972 had not been used within living memory; it was removed from the upper storey and placed outside when the roof was reslated in 1990.

Adjoining this present winch house is a large manual iron winch with Gothic detail, probably made by Toy, the Helston Founder. Henry Jane recalled its use: *"Long handles protruded on either side, one attached by a bearing into the winch-house wall. Ten men turned the handles to pull up the boats. It was last used in 1914 when the 1911 winch broke down for two days."*

The mechanical winch of 1911 was given to the cove by the landowner, Mrs Johnstone. Evergreens were obtained from the rectory to form an arch for the presentation, and to demonstrate the efficiency of the winch the 'Covers' great seine boat was decorated and hauled up the beach, filled with excited children.

Nineteen boats were to use it, fifteen crabbers, three seine boats of the 'Covers', 'Badgers' and Mr J Drews 'Mullet Seine Co.', and the pleasure boat of the Rev H Vyvyan. The Cadgwith Winch Committee met each month to discuss the condition of the Ruston Horrsley single cylinder engine, proposing repairs to be undertaken, agreeing on charges for its use, etc. In 1914 ring bolts, which still survive, along with massive iron chains, were fixed in the road to haul boats high up in bad weather.[10] In 1996 a new electric winch was installed.

Square Cellar – (Now Old Cellars Restaurant)

This large cellar with its wide south entrance, took its name not from its shape, but from its position adjoining the 'Square', an open area to the north. It was almost certainly built between 1780 and 1782 in conjunction with its associated capstan house, the present winch-house, and can be identified with the cellar named in a lease of 1799, in the period of investment by the Hawkins family:

> *"All those fish Cellars at Cadgwith, the linneys and Press Places whereof are about 14 feet deep and the cellar court about 28 feet long, 20 feet wide, over which are several dwelling houses in possession of John Randle, Richard Hichens and James Smith".*[11]

James Randle junior and Samuel Johns were the tenants at a yearly rent of £12.12s[12]

Sympathetically converted for use as a café in the 1975, it retains many of its original features, and still remains a traditional cellar. The central area retains its cobbled floor of beach pebbles, a feature known as 'caunsing'. Granite pillars support the lean-to roof on the western side, and lofts on the eastern side, where nets were once stored. The lease of 1799 shows that these same lofts were once used as dwellings. Later they probably provided temporary accommodation for helpers during the pilchard season. One was used as a 'Reading Room' in 1911 and they have all now been converted for use as holiday lets named 'The Old Cellars'.

Along the west wall is a stone projection beneath which press poles were wedged and placed over barrels, or 'hogs-heads'; below it is a wooden drain made from planks on which the latter were placed. As the cellar floor slopes gently to the south, it would have easily drained along this to a rectangular dreg-pit which survives in the south-west corner. Adjoining the latter was formerly a bark boiler and furnace, and here there is preserved a 'gurry', a fore-and-aft barrow once used to convey fish to the cellar.

On the exterior of the west wall is another projection for pressing, and still enclosed and protected by the lean-to roof of a more recent building. The area at the south entrance is known as 'The Town Hall', so named because of the fishermen's debates, which were held on the 'Stick' outside. This was once a barnacled covered mast from a wreck, providing a seat for the village 'parliament', but today it is a long plank. Henry Jane recalled that boys were "hit on the ear" if they lingered near the 'Stick', overhearing the fishermen's conversations!

The 'Stick' was described by a reporter in 1885:

> *"There is a bench right in the centre of the village, from which the whole of the little bay can be seen and from which the boat is watched that is perpetually on the look-out for signs of pilchards. On this bench the fishermen sit in patience, and wait for their harvest - they scarcely turn their eyes from the sea to look at the strangers who pass them."*[13]

On the left of the entrance to Square cellar the carved initials 'JFS 1908' can be identified with 'John F Stephens. Fisherman' of the 1861 and 1891 census reports, an experienced 'Huer', who has thus gained immortality!

'Western Capstan House' and 'Dummys Loft' – Both of these buildings lie beneath the Todden on the Grade side of Fishing Cove. The capstan house, lying nearest to the Todden, once served Dummy's Loft which lies beside it, and Badgers Loft, a large fish cellar which lies behind it. Today it is a dwelling, but it formerly housed a large wooden capstan in its upper storey which hauled up the five seining boats kept by the Badgers Seining Company.[14]

The wide slipway fronting the buildings has for long eroded away, and here also were the foundations of an old salt-house, where salt used in the bulking was stored. In the early years of this century the slipway was known as 'Billy's Slip' after the capstan house tenant Bill Jane.[15] A small iron winch still survives here.

Dummy's Loft is also now a dwelling. 'Dummy' is reputed to have been John Clark, a deaf mute who migrated to Cadgwith from England in search of work.[16] He was probably Michael Clark, a fifteen year old fisherman, recorded in the 1881 census report. In 1885, a Mr Barker of London presented Dummy, obviously then a pauper existing on parish relief, with a boat and fishing gear so that he could earn a living. When, in 1887, he saved from drowning two local men called Mitchell and Exelby, Mr Barker wrote to the local press urging them both to ensure that Dummy did not fall back on parish relief in the winter months.[17]

Badgers Loft – This fish cellar lies behind the Western Capstan House and Dummy's Loft, and could be entered from the road. It was once the cellar of the Badgers Seining Company, or 'Jeffreys Company'. In 1836 Richard Ivey occupied it.[18] The 1881 Ordnance Survey map shows it as a rectangular cellar with a courtyard at its centre. In 1972 it was in use as a garage and as a store for lobster pots. At that time a large fine bricked furnace, which concealed a copper boiler for boiling bark, survived in the north wall. Here also, in the upper section, was a brick pilchard

Main photograph:- Western Capstan House with seine boat and winch at centre. Dummy's Loft on right. Todden Cottage on left of group.

Winch outside Dummy's Loft. 1992 slipway now long eroded, seemai photograp

40

Main photograph 'Grade Side', Fishing Cove.
Left:- 'Long Loft' Note paved slipway with winch at
top in 'Little Cove'. Note sails drying and reservoir
on The Todden. (see inset)

Right:- Dolphin Cottage'
with fish cellar beneath,
Kiddleywink adjoining.
'Steamloft' right foreground

tank or 'steeping vat', built between granite pillars supporting the roof. Pilchards were kept here in brine, a method of curing introduced to Cadgwith in the 1880s, and superceding, to a great extent, the traditional method of placing the fish in bulk:

"It appears absolutely necessary that curers should abandon the old bulking process, and adopt the method of pickling in tanks and barrels. The old press-poles are also giving away to iron screws, which are more economical of room."[19]

This was in 1887, but we find no evidence of screw-presses being used at Cadgwith. There were also other pilchard tanks, but they had been destroyed by 1972. The building was converted to a cold-store for the fishery in 1998.

Steam Loft – This large building adjoins the stream in Fishing Cove, on 'Grade Side'. It was probably owned by the Badgers company, as two of their large seine boats were kept here – 'Mother Ivey' and 'Mosel';[20] the first was probably acquired from the seining company based at Mother Ivey's Bay, Padstow, which closed in 1879. 'Mosel' was named after the vessel, which was wrecked at Bass Point on 9th August 1882, when all of her 600 emigrants, 20 saloon passengers and 100 crew, were saved.

Granite pillars still support the roof on the west side, but the building was altered and heightened in 1881 to house two steam-powered seine-boats. This was not an innovation in Cornwall as a seine-boat had been adapted for steam at Sennen in 1870: *"A Sennen Cove seine boat is now at Penzance to be fitted with steam power, in order to shoot her nets."* She was named 'Ida' and in 1875 was *"in charge of, Mr Matthew Nicholas and a crew of three other men"*, lobster fishing at the Seven Stones.[21]

It was reported in 1881: *"Cadgwith. Two seine boats, intended for the pilchard fishery, made a trial trip on Monday last, from Falmouth to Cadgwith. The undertaking is in the hands of a company of Falmouth and London gentlemen, and Mr. John Cox, son of Mr Cox of Cadgwith is to be the manager."* All of the fish were to be brought to Falmouth, and sheds and stores were to be erected at Cadgwith: *"The two boats were built by Mr. H Lean of Falmouth and are a novelty in Cornish waters. They are 40 feet long with a 10 feet beam and are fitted with a pair of 6 cylinder engines. The boilers were supplied by Messrs. A.W. Robinson and Co. of the Victor Docks, London. They are of steel and are capable of 30 lbs pressure. The boats are also fitted with steam capstans and all the latest improvements."* New seines were also provided for use in deeper water.[22]

The roof of Steam Loft was raised because of the tall funnels, and on the Todden a reservoir (still extant) was built to fill the boilers of the vessels. Pipes conveyed water to it from the small stream which descends the hillside behind 'Long Loft', along the length of the Todden. The vessels were positioned beneath the reservoir and their boilers gravity-filled by hoses.[23]

The late Buller Arthur recalled them in 1973:

"My father was a crew member in one of the vessels; there were three men on each. They were fishing off the Rill, near Kynance, one day, when a gale blew up. Heavy seas washed the funnel away and she was, with difficulty, brought back to Cadgwith. They were not practical as their propellers fouled the nets when turning, so they were eventually used for crabbing".

This was certainly true, as on their first appearance at Cadgwith in Sept. 1881, the propeller fouled the seine net on the attempt to enclose a shoal of pilchards. A protector was hastily devised, and the second shooting of the net was a great success, securing four hundred hogsheads, which were later sold at Newlyn.[24] The Sennen steam vessel had also reverted to crabbing following complaints that her engine noise frightened the pilchards. [25]

Henry Jane recalled the walls of Steam Loft and other buildings at Fishing Cove festooned with Ray which were used as bait when dry.

Long Loft or Hounds Cellar – This large cellar, now converted to a dwelling, lies on a terrace above Little Cove. It was the premises of two seining companies known as 'The Hounds' and 'The Foxes'. Here a wooden floor sloped to a central channel from which the oil from the hogsheads of pilchards drained into a dreg-pit. When not in use, two large seine boats owned by this concern were hauled up the steep slipway, made of large boulders of serpentine, by a large iron winch. The remnants of another winch still exist above the slipway; the owner of Long Loft used it to haul up from vessels anchored or beached below, goods and commodities in baskets, which he subsequently sold within the village and at Ruan Minor etc.[26]

The cellar does not appear on the Grade Tithe Map of 1841 but was in existence by 1879. It was probably built in 1864 when it was reported, *"A large number of workmen are employed clearing out foundations for new stores in anticipation of increased trade."* [27] It was possibly the base of Messrs Sleeman.

The Kiddliwink and Dolphin Cottage – This large thatched building on 'Grade Side' consists of two cottages, 'Kiddliwink' on the north and 'Dolphin' on the south, and is one of the earliest buildings in Cadgwith, dating from the seventeenth century. There is a tradition that 'Kiddliwink', as the name suggests, was once a beer-house, whilst 'Dolphin Cottage' consisted of a dwelling above a fish cellar.

In 1972 the cellar floor of black pebbles, with its drains, still remained, but the dreg-pit had been filled prior to its use as a garage.[28] On the east exterior wall is a stone projection, beneath which press-poles were wedged for a run of hogsheads, protected by a lean-to roof. There are also connections with smuggling here. (See 'Smuggling' chapter)

The origin of the word 'Kiddleywink' was recorded in 1831. When some tinners called at a retail brewery near their mine, and asked for hot beer and sugar, the publican refused to serve them, but told them they could have the use of a room in a house nearby if they wish. There being no fire, or kettle in which to boil their beer and sugar, one offered to go to a cottage nearby to "get a kittle in a wink". The room was frequently, afterwards used by the recommendation of the brewer and by the tinners who named it 'Kittle in a Wink' afterwards abbreviating it to 'Kittlywink' or 'Kiddleywink'.[29]

BARKING NETS

In order to preserve the great seine net, tuck–net, etc, they were subjected to a process called 'Barking'. Although copper bark boilers with their furnaces were once a feature of all fishing concerns, references to the process are rare. In earlier times oak bark was used, but more recently the bark was called 'Cutch', a brown wood from Burma which came in boxes lined with the green leaves of the tree. In 1970 this writer recorded the process from a retired Mousehole fisherman, Mr. Jack Worth, then aged 70 yrs.

"The boiler was filled with water, the cutch chopped up like firewood, placed in a basket and then tipped into the large boiler over a furnace. When the cutch had dissolved and boiled, a tap at the bottom of the boiler was opened to allow the bark to flow into a vat set into the floor of the bark-house, which was all smoke, steam and voices.

The nets were stored in a loft above and one man fed them down through a trap-door above the boiler. Another fed it into the vat with an oar, and it was removed manually by a third man who pulled the net over a roller.

The bark was quite hot, so a bucket of cold water was kept handy so that hands could be plunged into it to prevent scalding. The net was then placed in a pile before being removed for drying – the surplus bark ran back into the vat."

This method was also used at Gunwalloe Fishing Cove where the vat remains.

The late Henry Jane recalled net-barking in Badgers Loft at Cadgwith:

"From a tap at the bottom of the boiler the bark ran in channels between the cobbled floor into a vat 6 ft deep, 6ft long and 4ft wide, sunk in the cellar floor. The nets were dipped for five minutes and then piled on the cobbles at one side of the vat, allowing the surplus bark to drain back into it."

A more detailed description of the laborious process was given in 1875, advising that oil and grease on nets be removed first by immersion and slow boiling for an hour, not allowing them to settle at the bottom of the boiler; then removing them over a boarded slope before tramping out as much water as possible before drying. They

were then barked by first boiling them for two hours with half a pound of best cutch per pound weight of nets and kept in the liquid for 48 hours.

When dry, they were plunged again into the same liquid with more water and a quarter pound of cutch added. When the nets were again dry, for the third time, they were washed in salt water, adding a gallon of limewater, made the day before from 14lbs of lime. The liquid which remained was increased by water until there were two gallons for each net section 100 yds in length and 15 score deep. Its preservative qualities were strengthened by two quarts each of Stockholm and gas tar, all kept to a slow boil, through which the nets were hauled. [1]

The process was obviously less complicated in the early years of the last century. The 'Old Fishermen's Bark House' lies on the north side of the Square, and was probably one of four barking places in Cadgwith in 1896, when cutch was used[2]. In 1972 remnants of the brick bark furnace remained there, whilst the copper boiler lay outside, discarded for scrap. The example in Square Cellar (Old Cellars Restaurant) was then complete, but has since been destroyed.

The word 'Bark' still survives in Cornish dialect when we refer to tea as sometimes being "as strong as bark"!

Tar was used to treat ropes.

THE TODDEN

'Todden' is Cornish for an area of grass, and at Cadgwith refers to the little peninsula which divides 'Fishing Cove' from 'Little Cove'. The 1841 Tithe Apportionment for Grade lists four houses here, inhabited by Henry Richards and others; these can be identified with four dwellings along the neck of the Todden mentioned in a lease of 1836 (see p13)

Fortunately the Todden forms a natural breakwater protecting Fishing Cove from the fury of winter storms. It has been said, "If the Todden goes, Cadgwith goes". Old photographs show that its summit was once much wider, and well grassed, but erosion has reduced its width considerably – at the southern end to about one foot; this is called 'Narrow Path', beyond which lies 'Island Rock', or 'The Island', and an isolated rock known as 'The Mare'.[1]

The Todden is pierced by a small cave named 'Todden Hole', which in rough weather becomes a blow-hole, shooting water with a thunderous noise half way across 'Fishing Cove'. On its summit is the reservoir once used for filling the steam vessels. Old photographs show a tall pole alongside it, which the late Henry Jane recalls was once used in launching the lifeboat in an operation called 'Lifeboat Outhaul'. A rope from the pole was attached to a large buoy anchored in Fishing Cove; the lifeboat was pulled down the beach and into the sea by a rope from the buoy passing over a pulley and block.

The Anthony Jane of the lease of 1836 can be identified with the common great-grandfather of both the late Henry Jane and Buller Arthur. He was described in the 1871 census as a 'Farmer of 10 acres', living on Grade side, and in 1891, when 75 years old, as 'Fisherman'. He was then affectionately named 'Granpa Atty', short for Anthony, and used the Todden as a rope-walk. The ropes were made of straw, or a special type of grass, using a 'wink' - a square of iron with a central cog working two others - the rope extending along the length of the Todden, to be used later for hauling crab pots.[2] Today the peninsula is used as a recreation area and as a vantage point for photographers.

THE DEVIL'S FRYING PAN

To the west of Cadgwith lies a collapsed sea cavern of some antiquity, first depicted in the Lanhydrock Atlas of 1696.[1] Since the nineteenth century it has been known as the 'Devil's Frying Pan', a name descriptive of the turbulence created by rough seas surging through its entrance. However, its ancient Cornish name was 'Hugga-Dridgee', *'hugga'* meaning 'cave', and *'dridgee'* or *'drigee'*, a derivation of *'trig'*, meaning 'low tide';[2] thus, 'tidal cave' describes this feature perfectly. Trigging was of course, the commonly practised custom of removing limpets at low tide.

In 1857 G Henwood wrote a series of articles describing the various geological features of the Lizard; he mentioned Cadgwith, and added that the Devil's Frying Pan resembled a volcanic crater, (some 2 acres in extent and 200ft deep) and was composed of huge blocks of serpentine of a finer quality than any on the coast. In the years 1818 - 1822, hundreds of tons of this were quarried there and taken to Bristol for crushing and the manufacturing of Epsom Salts, or sulphate of magnesia.[3] It was easily accessible by boats, in which the blocks of stone were taken to ships lying off in the bay. In 1851, several cargoes were still being shipped annually by the Penzance Serpentine Works, which was established in 1848[4], continuing a small business founded in 1827 by the grandfather of Mr J E Drew.[5]

SCHOOL DAYS AND RECREATION

During the early Victorian period many of the Cadgwith children would have received elementary education in the Sunday-schools of both church and chapels at Grade and Ruan. Henry Jane also spoke of a tradition that part of the loft above the present winch house was once used as a school. This can be verified, as in 1876 James Nicholls occupied *"the lofts called 'The Old School Room', and cellar underneath."*[1] This was probably a 'Dame's School', where the 'dame' taught her neighbours' children the basic rudiments of learning for a small sum of money.

A small schoolroom at Ruan Minor Churchtown was replaced in 1859 by a larger 'National School', run by the Church of England, to accommodate 80 pupils, with a principal room of 40ft by 17ft. Designed by J Piers St Aubyn on land donated by the Hawkins family, and helped by a government grant of £170, its foundation stone was laid on 12th August 1859 by the rector's son, Richard Jackson. The church choir sang and the playground was gaily decorated with flags supplied by John Ridge, the Chief Officer of the Cadgwith coastguards.[2] Its official opening, on 21st August 1860, was an equally festive occasion.[3]

In 1861 John Roberts of Cadgwith was a master there, along with schoolmistress Mary Trerise.[4] Mrs Georgina Hocking walked two miles daily to the school in 1907:

"We had a big school, nearly 100 children, but only two rooms to teach them in. In 1912 they built a classroom for infants, and one room was made into a cookery room… The seats on one side of the schoolroom were placed in a series of platforms rising up in steps; the small ones sat in the front and the bigger ones behind. We called it 'the Gallery'! I used a slate to write on at first, but I later used chequered paper".[5]

It had certainly been an era of change at the Churchtown, as preceding the building of the school, the ancient small church, which had been described as *"sadly dilapidated and in a disgraceful state of filth and decay"*, had been almost completely rebuilt in April 1855.[6]

Entertainment for Cadgwith folk was self-provided, with the new schoolroom at the Churchtown serving as a community hall. In January 1865 they trudged up Barn Hill, to see a charade, selections from 'Hamlet', 'The Merchant of Venice' and 'Othello': *"Most of the performers were workmen in Mr Cox's Serpentine Works"* at Poltesco.[7]

Madame Modjeska, the famous Polish actress stayed at the Cadgwith Hotel in 1880. She returned in August 1882 accompanied by her husband Count Bozenta and friends to give a repeat theatrical performance in the rectory grounds of St. Ruan before joining Lily Langtry on her American tour.[8] At this time it was reported, *"Every house in the neighbourhood is utilized for the convenience of summer visitors who are now arriving daily."*

Cadgwith had a cricket team at that period and, in July 1868, played the Helston 2nd eleven. The Rev P Robinson umpired for Cadgwith, *"who did no credit to the willow, having been brought out for 17 runs"*. They were again heavily beaten after dinner in a second innings, *"but enjoyed the tea which followed at the Cadgwith Hotel."*[9]

Their soccer skills were also lacking. When the 'Cadgwith Pilchards' played 'Kuggar Bulldogs' at Kuggar in 1904, they were beaten 5-0. The Cadgwith junior team later lost 7-0 to the Lizard Juniors![10]

The Cadgwith regatta was always a grand affair, with the Cove decorated with colourful flags provided by the coastguards. Pride of cove and parish was at stake when the rival fishermen of Church Cove, The Lizard, came to compete in rowing and sailing races, with as many as fifty boats entering. In June 1875, there were also skiff races, a duck chase, swimming races, and a greasy pole to be walked upon, extending from the Todden over the sea. The Mullion Band played music on the Todden.[11] In 1903 the

Churchtown, Ruan Minor C1910, note horse bus.

Lizard and Cadgwith regatta was held at Landewednack Church Cove, where crowds thronged the cliffs and were entertained by the Mullion Band.[12]

The Ruan Minor Wesleyan Sunday School festival was the event of the year for most Cadgwith children. The tea-treat, with its saffron buns and mugs of tea, was enjoyed by all ages. When, in June 1896, a poster at Cadgwith advertised the sermon and tea-treat, with prices 9d for adults and 6d for children, Mr George Tangye, the Cornish industrialist based at Birmingham, crossed the prices out, and wrote, "Free". This was confirmed, and on the day, the procession of 200 stopped at the post office and wired him a greeting,[13]

At that time the ancient custom of 'Colperra' still lingered in the Lizard peninsula, Mrs G Hocking recalled it still being practised in 1910:

"There was 'Colperra', on Shrove Tuesday, when some of the children collected eggs, slices of bread, jam and cream from the local farmers. Some would stay away from school that day. Our schoolmaster was a Mr Pyatt, from up-country, and when he called the register he would ask where they were. We would say "Gone to Colperra". Then he would say "I don't know how to spell that, so I'll put down 'Gone begging'" That was why most of us wouldn't do it. It died out after the First World War, when things were never the same again".[14]

Although the origins of the custom had by then been long lost, Colperra is said to have derived from the Cornish '*towl perow*' meaning 'crock-throwing', once a seasonal sport at The Lizard, known also as 'Lent crocking', when old pots, etc., were smashed.[15]

Many Cadgwith and Ruan Minor folk also picked or 'trigged' limpets on Good Friday, walking along the cliffs to Carleon Cove and Kennack Sands. In so doing they unknowingly continued the ancient pre-Reformation custom of eating fish, or shell fish on that holy day.

In 1911 a loft above Square Cellar, now a holiday flat, was converted for use as a reading room to be used by the fishermen and others. Certain regulations were proposed - men arriving after work had to wash their hands before playing cards, and there was to be *"No thumping on the table during card playing"*. Any member using bad language was banned for a week, and there was to be no spitting on the floor, as spittoons were provided - at one stage six more were ordered! Books, newspapers, tea and milk were provided for 1d a week, and no paper was to be held for longer than fifteen minutes. Sunday night services were held once a month from 8.00pm to 9.00 pm.[16.]

SMUGGLING

The remoteness of Cadgwith, and the coves of the Lizard peninsula made them ideal locations for landing smuggled goods. Contraband was easily brought from Brittany and France to be dispersed across the wide expanses of the downs of the Lizard, Predannack and Goonhilly, or concealed within the cottages and fish-cellars of Cadgwith.   The latter was populated chiefly by fishermen who knew the coastline intimately, and it was these, working in small groups, who enjoyed the bounty of 'Free trade'.

William Borlase wrote of this when briefly describing Ruan Minor in 1740;

"The parish is small, and lying on the sea, the people deal much in the Pilchard fishery, and for many in contraband to France for Brandy, Tea and the like. The arable land is very fruitful".[1]

By 1803 there had been no revenue officers resident in the coves of the area since 1799; before then each cove had its own officer, but all had died, and had not been replaced, thus leaving the whole Lizard peninsula unpatrolled. In 1803 Isaac Head wrote, in a petition, of the problems created by this situation,

"I observe that this port, independently of the harbour of Helford, contains within its limits five coves or creeks, viz. Porthoustock, Porthella and Coverack in the parish of St Keverne, Cadgwith in the parish of Ruan Minor, and Lizard in the parish of Landewednack, and that no Revenue Officer resides in either of the Coves aforesaid... that in each of the said coves an illicit trade for spirits, tea, tobacco, snuff, salt etc., is carried on to an extent almost beyond conception, to the great detriment of the Revenue."

The King's Preventive boat had been lying, useless, on the beach at Helford, incapable of being repaired because it had no maintenance. It was therefore asked,

"That a good boat to row and sail, properly equipped and manned, would, in conjunction with the Preventive Officers at the coves aforesaid, operate greatly in preventing smuggling being carried on to the enormous extent at which it is now affected."

With no officer in the coves, vessels could smuggle goods unchallenged; a boat had to be hired, and this, two miles from the place where cargoes were discharged; also, *"Vessels frequently discharge coals at the coves of Coverack and Cadgwith, both for the inhabitants of those coves and also for that of the Lighthouses at Lizard Point."* It was suggested that a Coal Meter be appointed.[2]

By 1815 Customs officers were residing at Cadgwith, almost certainly using a six oar gig which had generally found favour over cutters on the Cornish coast.[3] That February, *"Mr. Buck and the other Officers of the Customs, stationed at Cadgwith near Helston, seized 45 ankers of brandy on the beach near the former place".*[4] The following February Captain Buck *"succeeded in capturing a French vessel with 160 ankers of brandy on board."* The cargo was taken to the Custom House at Helston.[5]

Whilst dragging the sea off Cadgwith in March 1817, *"The Preventive boat at Cadgwith, found and seized about 150 ankers of brandy, which had been sunk in the sea near that place."*[6] By 1822 a Mr Bartlett was in command at Cadgwith, capturing a St. Mawes vessel *"with 120 kegs of contraband spirit".*[7] Yet more brandy was confiscated in 1842 when Lieutenant Josias Drew of the Revenue cruiser 'Dove' dragged up, or 'crept up', with grappling hooks, 95 kegs and linen, which were deposited in the 'seizure warehouse' at the Falmouth Custom House.[8]

In the early 1800s, two brothers made twenty-five smuggling runs from France to Cadgwith, where one of them lived. On one occasion the latter escaped the Preventive men by diving into the sea and hiding behind rocks where they could not follow.

When transporting the contraband by wagons, some were loaded, whilst others remained empty. The loaded wagons would lead, the empty ones following behind. If followed, on arriving at a junction in the track the latter would proceed rapidly, with much rattling and shaking, in another direction, pursued by the Preventive men.

"One of the brothers had a mare, trained for smuggling purposes. Her feet were muffled, and without a bridle, she would go along to the cliffs where the smugglers would load her with kegs, and send her off again. If she were caught the Preventive men would be told that she had been taken from her stable by someone."

On one occasion the Preventive men confronted one of the brothers with a search warrant at his Cadgwith cottage. An unsuccessful search was made, and an attempt at another being denied them, they drew their cutlasses to enforce it in the King's name. The Cadgwith man took his own cutlass from a beam, declaring they would have to pass him first. Upon their riding away to obtain another warrant, the

contraband was placed in a cellar, beneath a capstan, and the entrance concealed.[9]

Not only have such traditions been passed on in Cadgwith families, but, many cottages still retain places of concealment for smuggled goods. In 1976 the late Mr Buller Arthur showed this writer the site of a tunnel linking 'Dolphin Cottage' to his own, 'The Kiddleywink'. Beneath the former is an old fish cellar, now used as a garage; when a boy, Buller had been shown the entrance to the tunnel by an old fisherman. It was situated in the west wall, but has for long since been blocked up. He also knew of another tunnel, which runs from the old 'Bark House' in the Square, to a garden behind. In 1999 this was photographed by Jocelyn Jane; a trench-like excavation covered with large slabs of stone. Within it were numerous press stones complete with hooks.

When Mr Arthur was a child he often slept in his grandmother's cottage on the Todden, at the Westside of the cove. In the bedroom he would climb upon the top of the wall, where it met the sloping roof, to look down a shaft in the wall, which could be entered, feet first.

In 1974, when Mr Henry Jane was renovating a cottage on Barn Hill, leading to Ruan Minor, a loose stone was found to conceal a small cavity behind it. At 'Tregwyn', while removing old plaster, an alcove eight feet wide and three feet high

was revealed, approached by an undiscovered trapdoor in the attic space.[10]

Tim Goddard was present when men were working at 'Todden Cottage' in the early 1950s. A roof, or ceiling of a hidden room, with enough space for a boy to manoeuvre and stow away smuggled goods, collapsed. No doubt there are other smugglers' holes awaiting discovery. In 1986 Mr. Basil Bolitho of Vine cottage, Menavaur Walk, made the unusual discovery of a cloth bag hidden behind a wall of lathe and plaster, the latter bonded by horsehair. The bag contained several coins, including two of George III and the French Louis XV, both dated 1774. Other objects included a curved pocket knife, various buttons, etc. As the coins are worn, it would suggest a date of concealment, perhaps, in the mid nineteenth century.

The coastguards continued the role of the Preventive men at Cadgwith, thus further introducing new blood into the insular community. In the 1851 census report we find Lieutenant Joseph Robinson of the Royal Navy in charge, with six other coastguards, three Irish, two English and two Cornish. John Arkin was the Chief Officer in 1871, with six men to command, who lived on the Ruan and Grade sides of the cove. By 1891 all were listed under 'Coastguard Station' in Grade.

WRECKS AND WRECKING

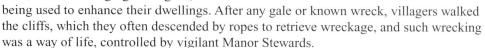

Cadgwith's situation, so near the hazardous rocks of the Lizard Point, the graveyard of so many vessels, meant that its fishermen, and those at Church Cove, were regularly engaged in both the saving of lives, and the salvaging of cargoes, some items being used to enhance their dwellings. After any gale or known wreck, villagers walked the cliffs, which they often descended by ropes to retrieve wreckage, and such wrecking was a way of life, controlled by vigilant Manor Stewards.

In 1837, Christopher H T Hawkins Esq., as 'Lord of the Manor of Trevethvas, Lucyas otherwise Rosewick' reaffirmed the area of coastline from which he enjoyed the right of wreck, *"On certain lands called Cadgwith alias Port Cadgwith. From the Lizard Cove westward to the Point called Point of Beast and eastwards to the extent of two fields belonging to the farm of Trethvas. Also from Cadgwith Cove eastwards to Poltesco. With other Lords, wreck in Kinance Cove and thence eastwards as far as the right of undivided property of the Lizard Downs extends"*.[1] At sea he could also, normally, claim any wreck as far as one could see a floating wine-cask. Any tenant declaring items would receive half the value of what had been found.

From the earliest times, and following the introduction of the Cadgwith lifeboat, 'Fishing Cove' frequently witnessed the landing of cold and soaked survivors of wrecks, who were subsequently afforded shelter, and provided for by residents before they moved on. One of the earliest-recorded of such scenes was in June 1826 when a schooner off the Lizard ran down the 'Young Ferdinand', from France bound for Brussels. The master drowned, but the crew took to its boats and landed at Cadgwith. Lieutenant Hooper, of the coastguard station there, went off with some boats and towed the wreck in, saving 300 casks of wine, before it was towed round to Falmouth for repairs.[2]

The distress of the East Indiaman 'Larkins', in November 1838, proved to be a blessing for the Cadgwith fishermen. The huge vessel, with a valuable cargo of indigo, saltpetre and silks, had struck heavily on the Seven Stones,

Coastguards with Anthony Jane on right in white coat. C1900 (per Jocelyn Jane)

near Scilly, causing her to leak badly. Her Captain, Ingram, proceeded to Penzance in a Scilly pilot boat where he obtained fifty hands to help man the pumps; they set off to assist the vessel, but failed to find her.

In the meantime, the 'Larkins' had reached Coverack, en route to Falmouth, when Mr James, a licensed pilot, heard her signal guns and boarded her. When off the Lizard, he sent word ashore for men to man the pumps; twenty-eight Cadgwith men responded, and assisted by the crew of HMS Meteor, a Packet steam vessel, successfully brought the ship into Falmouth.[3] It was later reported, *"The Cadgwith boatmen, 28 in number, who assisted this ship into port, have received £300 between them for their services. Mr James, the pilot, and two men employed in his cutter are paid £100; the coastguard officer to receive £250".*[4]

Cadgwith Lifeboat Record Board when at Aero Park, (Flambards) l-r:- Henry Jane (ex-coxswain), J.C. Trewin. Arthur Willey (Launcher), Mayor of Helston, Richard 'Buller' Arthur. (Photo D. Jory)

It was not until 1859 that a lifeboat was placed at the Lizard, and in 1867 another was positioned at Cadgwith to assist them. The self-righting lifeboat 'Western Commercial Traveller' was presented by a group of that name and launched by the wife of the rector of Grade and Ruan on 12th September 1867. It was 33ft long with ten oars.

The crew of ten, selected from twenty volunteers, took their places in the boat dressed in dark blue Guernsey frocks and red woollen hats, and were taken to sea by Captain Ward who instructed them how to fire two life rockets as a spectacle for the crowd of spectators.[5]

She was first used that November when permission was granted to save a huge and valuable seine-net. A large shoal of pilchards had been enclosed, but the wind had risen during the night, preventing the fish being taken. The net eventually split and the fish escaped. The lifeboat crew successfully prevented it from drifting away by using a grapnel.[6]

In March 1869 it was reported that the lifeboat had been out for the third time that year, aiding the crew of the 'Frances and Ann'. The lifeboat men had been awarded a donation by the Lloyds Association, for rescuing eight people from the 'Calcutta', of £8.15s.4d each, which was presented in the schoolroom at Ruan Minor.[7]

In 1878 the lifeboat was renamed the 'Joseph Armstrong' after the Chief Superintendent of the Locomotive and Carriage Department of the Great Western Railway. She was quickly on the scene in fog and rain in September 1879 when the Cunard vessel 'Brest', bound for Liverpool with 130 European emigrants for New York, thirty-four crew and five stowaways, went aground between Church Cove and Polbarrow.

There was great panic as people threw themselves into the sea to reach the lifeboat and fishing boats, which also assisted. Forty passengers were landed at Cadgwith in two trips by the lifeboat, where they received shelter, food and clothing. Later they refused to travel to Falmouth by tug, being so afraid after their previous experience, and preferred to walk the twenty miles![8]

The first 'Joseph Armstrong' was replaced in 1887 by a larger vessel, 37 feet long with twelve oars, bearing the same name. In June 1893 a surprise annual practice was described,

"On Tuesday night the little fishing village of Cadgwith, near the Lizard, was the scene of considerable excitement. Shortly before 10 'o'clock two rockets (the well known signal for a wreck), broke upon the stillness of the night air, and roused the inhabitants. In a moment lights twinkled in every window, and in an incredibly short time the space in front of the lifeboat house was filled with men, many still huddling on their clothes. Without the slightest confusion, some quickly placed the trucks, others cleared a passage on the beach, while the crew donned their corked jackets, and on the word of command of the coxswain, and amidst the shouts of the helpers, the huge form of the 'Joseph Armstrong' crashed down the shelving beach, and 13 minutes from the time the signal had fired the boat was in the water".[9]

In 1900 the 39ft long twelve oar 'Minnie Moon' took over, followed by 'Herbert Sturmy' in 1936, and the 'Guide of Dunkirk' in 1941.

The reserved manner of the quietly spoken Cadgwith men belied their incredible bravery in venturing forth into dense fogs and mountainous seas. When the Cadgwith lifeboat station closed in May 1963, a total of 388 lives had been saved. Its record board can be seen at the Old Cellars Restaurant (Square Cellar). A new lifeboat station was built at Kilcobben. Many items were salvaged from local wrecks and still survive locally. Mr Buller Arthur recalled,

"The 'old men' went wrecking using 'wrecking tongs'; this was a pole about 16 feet long, at the end of which was a pair of tongs, one immoveable, the other moveable. Attached to the latter was a length of rope, which passed along the handle and when pulled, closed the tongs. It was used, sometimes with a water glass, to retrieve copper piping, and other valuable items".

Mr Henry Jane spoke of his grandfather having been blinded when wrecking. This must have occurred in 1858, as it was reported then, *"Henry Jane of Cadgwith, and Edward Carter of the Lizard, while working on the wreck of the 'Zebra', have each lost the sight of an eye by means of loosing rivets."*[10] This Henry had handed on a powder horn decorated with wigwams etc., which he had salvaged from either the 'Marianna', or 'Nouvo Raffaelino', two Genoese barques wrecked at the same time at the Lizard in 1872. Lamps, plates, furniture, and timber for building all somewhat recompensed for the saving of lives. Henry Jane recalled many wreck sales in Cadgwith as a boy, when huge sails of thick canvas stretched across the shingle of Fishing Cove, *"when wet, as heavy as steel"*. It was a similar scene in September 1809 when articles salvaged from the wreck of the sloop 'Jennet' were auctioned- eight large sails, *"Main, Try, Gib, Fore, Gaff and Square sails"*, rigging and masts, timbers etc., littered the cove.[11]

Henry's wife, Irene, born in 1913, recalls the wreck of the 'Clan Malcolm' in September 1935, a 5994-ton steamer that went aground in fog at Green-Lane Cove near the Lizard: -

"I and some friends were at the scene in the morning, sat on the cliffs waiting for the fog to lift. When it did, it was the funniest sight I've seen. The boat was just off shore, and there, still on its derricks, was a lifeboat full of Lascars (Indians) who peered from beneath a tarpaulin with wide, wild eyes! They were later brought into Cadgwith – the English in spats, collars and ties"

The lifeboat house remains, now housing the Cadgwith Pilot gig. Drowned wreck victims were placed, temporarily, in the adjoining coastguard gig-house. A new building was donated in 1891 by Joshua Sydney Davey of Bochym, one of the principal landowners, whose monogram, and the date, appeared in granite above the entrance. In recent years it was removed when a window was inserted during its conversion to a shop. It can now be seen built into a cottage at Barn Hill. The coastguard watch house stands at the cliff edge above Fishing Cove; in 1905 plans to replace the lookout there with a hut and flagstaff at Enys Point were abandoned.[12]

The coastguards had traditionally lodged with Cadgwith families, or had rented cottages, their expenses paid by the Admiralty. In 1867, Mary Randle of Helston rented them a cottage of six rooms, three of them bedrooms, *"the seventh house in the road leading to the Watch House"*, (Menavaur Walk) at £8 yearly.[13] By 1891 they were living in a still extant row of coastguard houses, built above the cove on Grade side.

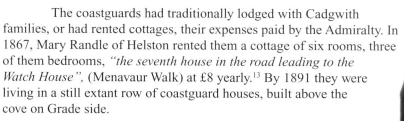

Coastguard Watch House.
Top:- 'The Guide of Dunkirk'.
(per Gerald Luke)

POLTESCO

The National Trust owns Poltesco and Carleon Cove. Well wooded, with a wide and fast-flowing stream descending to the sea, it is a peaceful and idyllic spot, belying its former importance as an industrial site for the fishing and serpentine industries. Its history possibly extends from the remote Iron Age as 'Carleen' means 'fort of slab-stones'. The small property on the Cadgwith side of the valley was known as 'Carlyen' in 1539,[1] so one could expect it, possibly, to have been the site of an oval or circular earthwork with a defensive bank and ditch, giving its name also to the cove below.

There is also here the ancient mill of Poltesco, its machinery and water wheel lovingly restored in recent times by millwright Mr Anthony Unwin. We find "The Mill of Poltuska" mentioned during the reign of Richard II (1367 – 1400 AD).[2] Carved on one of its interior walls is a figure of Christ crucified, and nearby, the initials of William Wearne, the miller here in 1878.[3] On the exterior, a series of millers carved their initials and dates in the 18th century; one was Bernard Rutter, 1790, forbear of Henry Rutter, miller there in 1856, and Solomon who succeeded him in 1861.[4]

In 1738 George Roberts took the lease of both 'Carlean Great Croft' and 'The Carleans', part of Treworder Wollas, with its dwelling house barns etc. Two of the conditions of his lease were that he and his under-tenants *"will grind all his and their corn and grain which shall grow, at the Mill or Mills of the said Manor of Trethvas, Lutyas and Rosweth called Polteska Mills"*, and he was to *"send an able man out every year to clean and scour the Conduits, Leates and Pools belonging to the said Mills"*.[5]

Adjoining the mill is the quaint bridge bearing the date 1802, and the letters 'G' and 'R', the stream here dividing the parishes of Grade to the east and Ruan Minor to the west.

CARLEEN FISH CELLAR

The site later chosen for a serpentine factory at Poltesco, or Carleon Cove, in Grade parish, had for long been occupied by a typical rectangular cellar of the pilchard fishing industry, which is shown on the Lanhydrock Atlas of 1695.[6]

In 1809, the 'Endeavour' and Lizard seines were reported to be *"lying at Carleen cellars"*, and consisted of two Stop and Tuck seines, two new seine boats, one

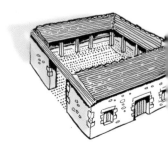

Typical Fish Cellar

new Carrying boat, and 400 bushels of salt. Another report, in 1812, shows that the Lizard Fishery was still based there and had, *"three Stop and one Tuck seines, three seine boats, one Carrying boat, and two Lurkers, together with a new Barking Furnace and seine cabins"* – all auctioned at that time.[7]

POLTESC

Site of present Carleon House (1861)

Fish Cellar

The cellar was still in use in 1838 when *"10 16ths parts, or shares in the Pilchard Sean at Carleen, near Cadgwith"* were advertised for sale. It then consisted of *"Two Stop and one Tuck Seans, two Sean boats, two Followers, and a large Carrier, almost new, with a full stock of warps, grapnels, and other requisites, and a corresponding interest in the cellars and cellar materials, and about 500 Bushels of Salt."* Mr. Bernard Rutter, possibly the Poltesco miller, was available to show the seine to prospective share buyers.[8]

Capstan House

In August 1840, 130 hogsheads of pilchards were taken at Carleen, [9] but the erection of a new fish-cellar, still extant, at Church Cove, Landewednack in 1837-1838, by Sir Charles Hawkins, perhaps eventually prompted the seiners, to re-establish their industry there, where it had previously thrived, thus abandoning the ancient cellar at Carleon Cove. [10]

CARLEON COVE 1841

In 1841 William Jose held the lease of the seaward end of the valley,[11] and the cellar, which was converted to a large serpentine factory in about 1848.

Today, we can see the great, almost circular, capstan house of serpentine, with its blocked opening, from which the capstan rope emerged to haul the heavy seine boats up the slipway. The latter is probably represented by the adjoining track, which would have also been used by farmers to obtain sand and seaweed for manure from the cove.

THE LIZARD SERPENTINE COMPANY, POLTESCO

The Lizard is famous for its serpentine rock, which, when polished, displays its bright colours of green and red. We do not know when it was first used commercially to make small items, but in 1853 it was reported that the brackets of two monuments in Westminster Abbey, erected in 1710 and 1711, and also the panel bordering of the monument erected by the Marquis of Halifax in memory of his friend Addison, the poet, were of serpentine.[12] J E Drew of the 'Cornish Serpentine Marble Manufactory, Penzance', first manufactured *"cheap but ornamental articles"* in 1827.[13]

The Rev C A Johns in his work 'A Week at the Lizard' (1848) makes no mention of a serpentine factory in the area, but does refer to the tradition of individuals producing small items, noting that many of the Preventive men at Cadgwith *"spend a considerable part of their leisure time in polishing specimens of serpentine… which they found on their coastal patrols"*.

In September 1846, Queen Victoria, Prince Albert and their children, visited Mounts' Bay in the Royal yacht. The Prince landed at Penzance, and whilst touring the Geological Museum there, was shown specimens of polished serpentine. His enthusiasm was such that, on the return journey to Falmouth, he was rowed ashore at Kynance Cove, where on seeing the sea-polished stone in its natural state, he exclaimed, *"The Queen MUST see this!"* The barge *"accordingly returned for her Majesty and the Royal children, who were equally gratified with the Prince"*.[14]

They might also have seen the large water wheel at the bottom of the valley *"employed to turn the rude machinery by which some works in the serpentine are affected, but these are on a small scale"*. The inhabitants of some small cottages there were employed in collecting specimens of serpentine and steatite, forming them into pedestals, tazzi, candlesticks, brooches and bracelets etc. that they sold to visitors.[15]

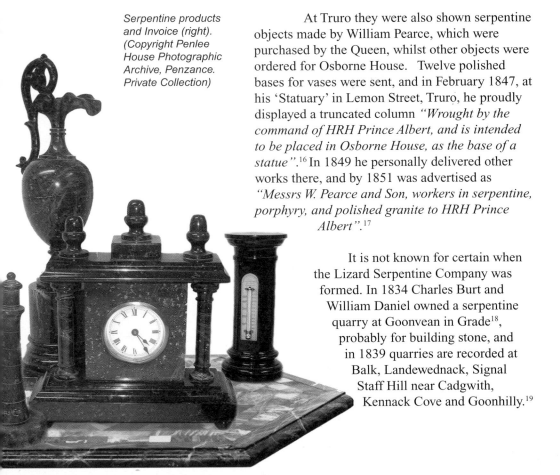

Serpentine products and Invoice (right). (Copyright Penlee House Photographic Archive, Penzance. Private Collection)

At Truro they were also shown serpentine objects made by William Pearce, which were purchased by the Queen, whilst other objects were ordered for Osborne House. Twelve polished bases for vases were sent, and in February 1847, at his 'Statuary' in Lemon Street, Truro, he proudly displayed a truncated column *"Wrought by the command of HRH Prince Albert, and is intended to be placed in Osborne House, as the base of a statue"*.[16] In 1849 he personally delivered other works there, and by 1851 was advertised as *"Messrs W. Pearce and Son, workers in serpentine, porphyry, and polished granite to HRH Prince Albert"*.[17]

It is not known for certain when the Lizard Serpentine Company was formed. In 1834 Charles Burt and William Daniel owned a serpentine quarry at Goonvean in Grade[18], probably for building stone, and in 1839 quarries are recorded at Balk, Landewednack, Signal Staff Hill near Cadgwith, Kennack Cove and Goonhilly.[19]

In 1876 it was reported that the company was formed "about" 1848.[20] It would appear that they were at first merely quarrying the serpentine to supply not only William Pearce of Truro, but the larger Penzance Serpentine Company which built a factory there, at Larrigan, in 1847; in fact, it was stated in 1853, that the first to work serpentine on a large scale was Mr John Organ, manager of the Penzance concern, *"both on the beach and in a quarry, long before Messrs Brace and Colt, who were the second parties on the ground".*[21] No doubt, those at Poltesco realised the advantages of building a similar factory near the source of the serpentine, thus greatly reducing transportation costs.

Mr Anthony Unwin, one-time millwright at Poltesco, informs this writer that a small mill which he excavated in the farm-yard there, was, according to local tradition, the first serpentine factory. The site of the second factory at Poltesco, or Carleon Cove, was well chosen. The old fish-cellar was converted to a factory, and a wide and fast-flowing stream provided water, diverted into an aqueduct, to turn a large water-wheel, which powered various lathes and saws.

With the great success of the Penzance Serpentine Company at the Great Exhibition of 1851, which attracted orders from Prince Albert, the Prince of Prussia and the aristocracy, and with the praise of prominent architects supporting its adaptability for outside use and brilliancy of polish,[22] the success of the Poltesco industry was assured.

In order to produce columns, and other architectural features, deeper quarrying was necessary to obtain superior material. Powerful derrick cranes were introduced, and in October 1852, the largest block of red serpentine yet to be hewn was obtained from a quarry at Kennack, 9 feet in length, 6ft in width, and 3ft in depth: - *"Still larger blocks will be extracted from the quarries hereafter, as the latter are extending more into the country, and the serpentine there is sounder and better capable of being procured in more massive pieces than when near the sea".*[23] The quarries were about 60 feet deep *"and the serpentine is removed from its place by the aid of wedges and lifting jacks, as blasting would seriously injure the material."*[24]

65

By 1855 the company had show rooms at 20, Surrey Street, The Strand, and another at Poltesco.[25] Henry Cox, a Lincolnshire man who had settled at Cadgwith, was manager at the factory in 1856, with William Pearce who owned the serpentine business at Truro, and who was now employed here for his expertise. By 1861 Frederick Smith, an experienced marble-turner had been sent for from Derbyshire, along with William Harris, a marble and stone mason, from Devonport, to use their skills alongside local Cornish workers.

© Penlee House Photographic Archive Penzance.

Serpentine Turners

In that year, there was a need to expand the business because of demand. Henry Cox thus invited tenders "For building a New Factory and Cottage for the Lizard Serpentine Co. at Poltesco". [28] Thus, the old fish cellar was extended, and 'Carleon House' built as the manager's residence.

That October the Lizard Serpentine Company's steam vessel, Foyle, carrying a valuable cargo of serpentine articles for London, which included a mantelpiece valued at one hundred guineas, sank at Falmouth; it was fortunately raised, and the cargo was saved. [29] It is perhaps this incident, which gave rise to the story of the loss of a valuable cargo of serpentine goods, leading to the demise of the industry here. Mr Anthony Unwin once recorded from an elderly resident that finished articles, packed in 'elephant grass', were ferried out from the wharf at high tides, in shallow-draft barges to vessels anchored off shore. The barges were kept alongside the surviving wharf fronting the factory ruins. Gales frequently piled up boulders in the channel to the sea, creating unwanted labour in their removal.

In 1864 the factory's 25ft-diameter water-wheel was powering the machinery, and the company had £10,000 capital.[30] It was probably the demise of the 'London and Penzance Serpentine Company' of Wherry Town, Penzance in 1865,[31] which created an increase in trade at Poltesco, prompting the use of steam power. This was introduced in 1866, when tenders were invited for building "a boiler house, stack, and other

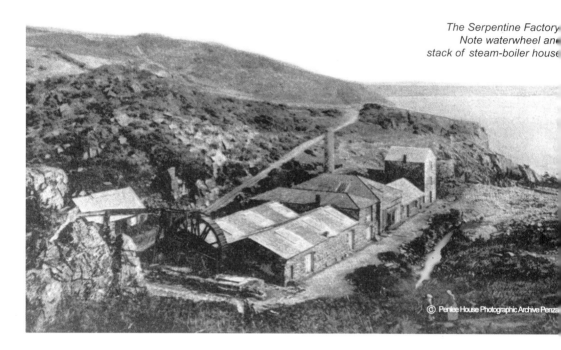

The Serpentine Factory
Note waterwheel and
stack of steam-boiler house

© Penlee House Photographic Archive Penza

outbuildings of stone, wood, and slate; also framework erections for travellers".[32] The latter, cranes moving along tall gantries, were used to transfer large blocks of serpentine around the site. The surviving warehouse of three floors, adjoining the old fishery capstan-house, formed a part of this new complex, and still bears its date stone, 'LSC 1866' (Lizard Serpentine Company).

It was surprising that, in 1871, with orders amounting to £10,000 the business was sold to a company formed with a capital of £15,000 in £1 shares to become the 'Poltesco Serpentine Marble Company'. They acquired six quarries and the rights of quarrying over 750 acres, along with the factory and machinery, on which £20,000 had been expended. With the highly productive quarries a profit was ensured if only building stone was produced, and the increased popularity of serpentine beyond the Tamar, delivered in the market for about one third of the price of foreign marbles, should have resulted in high returns.[33] It was therefore surprising that in 1876 the

Directors, Lieut. Col. Innes, Capt. G E Hill, the Hon. H J Coke and Mr S R Lewis, sold the business by auction. There were no bids for parts of the quarrying, or for the factory and cottage, but a 20hp horizontal engine was sold to Messrs Trevithick and Co. for £100, and a boiler for £25.[34] These, and a list of the machinery in the factory, enlighten us as to the system of production; "15 Lathes, Circular Sawing machine, 3 Ripping frames, 2 Circular Polishing Machines, Automatic or self polishing machine, complete, Cast Iron Float with working gear, 2 Sawing Machines with 4 large sawing-frames, New framework for 2 large saws (never used), Powerful Traveller with 2 tramways 90 yards long, 3 Fox and Henderson's cast iron patent winches, Toy's patent screw-jacks, Traveller crane by Taylor and Son of Birmingham, Railway Trucks etc., Smith's Forge complete for two, Avery's patent weighing machine. The stock of railway-iron, steel, brass, stone, coal, about 30 tons of quarried stone, Office fittings, Household furniture etc."[35]

It was estimated that about £120,000 had been expended over a chequered period of 28 years (1848). [36] The factory remained idle until 1878 during which period local shops suffered greatly due to a shortage of cash-flow in the area. It was then leased to Jabez Druitt, a Londoner experienced in the cemetery monumental trade. He took as his manager, John Nankervis of Newlyn, who had probably gained his experience with the Penzance Serpentine Company.[37] In 1877 John had been presented with the Freedom of the Turner's Company, and a silver medal, for producing a serpentine tazza – a saucer-shaped cup mounted on a foot.[38]

Unfortunately, by 1881 there was less demand by architects, partly due to a difficulty in meeting their orders promptly because of the lack of stones of the requisite size. Druitt introduced numerous improvements, including a new water-wheel built by Toy, the Helston Founder, in order to hasten production. The company was now to experience a high degree of success, using material from six quarries – Signal Staff near Cadgwith, Treal Quarry, Balk Quarry at Landewednack, Long Alley near Ruan Major Church, Poltesco and Killawyn. The serpentine from the latter was of a rich jet black, and from the others a beautiful black and red with green intermixes. Workers carefully removed the stone using wedges and lifting jacks; powerful cranes hoisted the serpentine blocks onto large wagons, drawn by ten horses, to be conveyed to the factory.[39] It was dangerous work, as Peter Thomas was crushed to death whilst moving out a large block in 1866.[40] A Mr Ellery of Grade held the haulage contract for both the raw material and the finished goods, which were taken to Penryn and Falmouth at the rate of £1 per ton, to be shipped to British ports, France, America, India, Australia, etc.[41]

Twenty men and three boys were employed at the factory in 1883. There the great blocks were placed under a saw-frame, of which there were five, each with sixteen saws; water and sand were continually applied to the latter, which sawed at about three inches in ten hours. Once cut into slabs, the serpentine was moved by a travelling crane on a gantry and stored until needed. There was also a large sanding bed, three polishing beds, six turning lathes, and numerous circular saws, all powered by the large water-wheel and by steam.

Carleon House   Crane Gantry   Steam Boiler House.   Warehouse. Coal Stor to right, previously th Capstan House.

© Penlee House Photographic Archive Penzance

Once cut to the required length, a rough copy of the design was made, using a hammer and chisel, before being shaped on a revolving lathe by the 'cutter'. The 'Grounder', working another lathe, removed the rough surface of the stone using sand and flint, then a finer sand, wash leather and emery powder, before being finally polished with various oils, crocus and corduroy.[42]

In 1891, according to the census, the latter was done by Samuel Willis of Plymouth, living at Poltesco, 'Marble Polisher', whilst James Harris, also of Poltesco, was described as 'Serpentine Marble Turner'. Articles were then placed in the showroom where John Nankervis conducted visitors throughout the year. Shafts, slabs etc. cost about 4s 6d per foot, and handsome chimney pieces from £3.10s each in 1883.[43]

Several workmen travelled to Paris in 1884 to supervise the erection of a new shop front.[44] Two years later a fourteen day exhibition was held at Poltesco, which included a large pulpit with four green columns and entered by five steps of black and red serpentine.[45]

In 1893, Poltesco serpentine was said to be superior to that found in North America. Some years previously a parcel of rough samples were forwarded to the Smithsonian Institute in America where they were cut and polished and used in a system of exchanges.[46] Despite its success, cheaper marble products from Italy and Spain appear to have proved a fatal blow to the industry, and in April 1893, Jabez Druitt, of the "Lizard Serpentine Marble Works", placed the lease on the quarries and factory for auction. The machinery was again listed along with "ten beautifully polished mantelpieces, seven fenders, a church lectern, five large bust pedestals, columns, 10,000 feet of sawn slab from 1½ inches to 12 inches thick etc."[47]

The factory was never re-opened. The valley was again silent. No more the rasping of saws, the whirring of lathes, the rumbling of the traveller crane, the shouts of carriers urging teams of sweating horses drawing heavy timbered wagons. The deserted building was used as a carpenter's shop, and the water-wheel to power a chaffing machine for horse feed until its removal in about 1917. In 1923 the works were demolished.[48] Today, only a few walls remain, along with the water-wheel pit, and a section of the boiler-house stack. The wharf, and slabs of serpentine survive, the latter, still bearing grooves created by steam-powered saws. Towering above all, is the warehouse, alongside the old capstan house of the 'Carleen Fishery'. The little bungalow of 1861, 'Carleon House', once the residence of the factory manager, with its stable of brick, remains intact. Within the former is a mantelpiece of red serpentine, as a testimony to a once proud industry. The whole valley became the property of the National Trust in 1990, due to the bequests of Miss Margaret Ironside of Wadebridge and Miss Nita Cohen.

Fortunately the production of serpentine continues at Church Cove and at the Lizard, where individuals make small items for tourists.

CADGWITH FISHING DIALECT

The plank bench, 'The stick', at the front of Old Cellars Restaurant, was, until some years ago, the meeting place of elderly Cadgwith fishermen, who in their final years sat in the sun and reminisced of days gone by. Their conversation, in rich dialect, is now a thing of the past. In 1973, this writer sat with them on several occasions, all then between sixty and seventy years of age, and recorded those words associated with fishing. Richard Buller Arthur (1908-1981), the source of no less than sixty-nine words, stated that he had heard them frequently used before the First World War, and to a lesser degree until the 1930s.

Such dialect words varied from cove to cove, harbour to harbour, many stemming from the Cornish language. Although most were recorded by Robert Morton Nance before 1920, it is of interest to illustrate their survival, along with others hitherto unrecorded. The meanings are as given by the speakers, and the Cornish translations are from 'A glossary of Cornish Sea Words' by R. Morton Nance, edited P A S Pool, 1963.

L to r:- 'Doctor' Cook Stephens, Tommy Jane, Fred Stephens, Lewis Jane ('Chink') with daughter, Ball Jane and Bert Willey.

BALK – A huer's lookout on a cliff for shoals of pilchards.

BREEDING – To make nets.

BUCKLER – A wooden cover which goes inside a barrel, or hogshead of pilchards when being pressed.

BUGS – Small hen crabs ('u' as in 'should').

BULDRANG – A small ling like fish with spots, found in rock pools

BULK – A built up pile of salted pilchards, before pressing

BULL-RAA – a small wrasse.

BULLY – A large pebble.

BULTER – A long line of hooks for catching conger, ling etc.

BUTTONS – a small starfish.

CAIRN – A rocky-bottomed fishing ground.

CANKER – A small crab (Cornish).

CANNY KEER and CANNYCREEPER – A spider crab (Cornish Nance gives canker hyr-y-baw, long-clawed crab).

CATER – Small wooden frame for winding fishing lines (rhymes with 'Crater').

CAUNCE – A stone paved area, or way.

CHILL – a lamp which burned fish-oil or 'train-oil'.

CHIM – the base of a lobster pot.

CLAVE – A wooden stand for long lines to keep fish hooks clear.

COBBYHEADED – A tufted sea-bird.

COLPRES – A wooden lever.

CRUTCHES – Rowlock pins.

CUFFA – A hen crab.

DAWL – A tangled heap – as of rope.

DRANG – a narrow channel along the seashore.

ETTER – A long shackle shaped iron implement used for winching up boats on a beach.

FERMADE – A salted and pressed pilchard.

FIVE FINGERS – A starfish.

FUNNEL – the entrance, or mouth, of a lobster pot.

GAAVER or GAYVER – A 'craw fish', or crayfish (Cornish. Nance gives gavar, a goat, a shortened form of gavar-mor, sea goat).

GAVERICK – Spider crab (Nance gives from Cornish gevryk, little goat).

GERRICK – A garfish.

GINJIN – A fine copper wire for fastening to fish hooks. (Hard G).

GLIT WEED – Fine seaweed that adheres to nets.

GROBMAN – A small type of bream. (Cornish. Nance gives Cornish cromman later crobman, a sickle).

GULDERN – Layers of twine, approx 6 inches, fastened to old type conger-hook.

GULNIGAN – A cuttle fish gaff. (Cornish. Nance gives Cornish gwelen-hyk = Hook rod).

GULYARK and GULIARK – A small velvet harbour crab, with flat legs for swimming. (Cornish. Nance gives Cornish culyak, a worthless creature or cul y aryk, with a lean little leg).

GURRY – A hand-barrow for carrying fish.

GUTHEN – An underwater ledge, or rock. (Cornish. Nance gives Cornish cudhen in mutation gudhen, a hidden rock just under the water.

HEVVA – The alarm cry, shouted by the 'Huer' when pilchards are sighted. (Cornish. Nance says contracted form of old Cornish hedva, swarming or flocking).

HUBBA – Variant of Hevva.

JACKS – Cock crabs.

JOUSTER – A fish hawker.

KIEVE – A wooden tub.

KILLICK – An anchor for small boats. (Cornish. Nance gives culyek, cock, from its spurs in the form of flukes).

Got any long goose 'ast tha ?

'Ave a scrowler me 'ansome !

Tha' ol' chill ded'n 'av any train in un !

Gracie's gone out tryg limputs.

Some 'ansome paddy linkum, inna ?

Gib me some snead cust tha ?

LANTERN – Megrim, a small fish
LEGH – A flat rock on the shore. (Cornish, flat).
LONG GOOSE – A crayfish (French, *Langouste*).
MARGLE – Coral, coagulation.
MORREPS – Moorland by the coast.
MEAN – Rock, used in rock names (Cornish).
MERL – A link of chain (Nance gives Old French *merel*, counter).
MENNIS – A grooved mooring stone for fishing gear etc. (Cornish. Nance gives *men-nos*, mark stone).
MULLY – Blenny, found in rock pools. Rhymes with Bully. (Cornish. Form of *mulleygranack*, sea toad (Nance)).
MURR – Guillemot.
MURGY – A spotted dogfish. (Cornish. Nance gives *mor*, sea, and *ky*, dog)
PADDY LINKUM – A starfish.
PADDY LINKUM – A small squid. (Cornish. Nance gives Cornish *padel* = ink-pot, *ynk* from English ink. Ink fish or great cuttle fish).
PENTAGIZZA – A small rock ling. (Cornish).
PESSACK – A decayed salted pilchard (Cornish. Nance gives Cornish *pesak*, rotten).
PLUMZUGEN – Bearded rock ling. (Cornish. Nance gives Cornish *plumsugan* meaning either 'Plum juice'(referring to the colour of the fish) or 'Suck a plum' (referring to its mouth).
PREEN – A forked wooden skewer used in baiting crab pots. (Nance gives Old English *preon* meaning pin).
QUEAL – A coil, as of rope. (Nance gives Breton *kuilma*, to coil).
RILL – A coastal cleft.
RUN – A line of hogsheads being pressed.
SCANTEL – A flat wooden measure for braiding nets, mending (Cornish. Nance gives Cornish *scantlyn*, a measure).

SCROWLER – A pilchard split open and dried in the sun. (Also, Scrowled over an open fire in a Scrowling Iron. (MT)).
SCODMANS – Bits and pieces, wooden bits of wreckage etc, (Cornish. Nance gives Cornish *skobman*, splinters of wreck).
SEW (SUE) – To dry up. Above the tide on the shore.
SHEEVE – To row a boat by pushing the oars in front of you.
SKEET – A long tear in a fishing net. (Cornish. Nance gives SKATE from Cornish *sketh*, tatter.
SNEAD – A ribbon of fish as bait. (Nance gives Old English *snaed*, a morsel cut off).
SOWAN – A gully in a cliff, roofless cave, or hole in a cliff. (Cornish. Form of ZAWN, Cornish *saun*).
STEEVES – Bent willow bars in crab pots.
SWAISE – To wave the arms as a signal.
TAMLYN – A young cod.
TARROCK – A kittiwake or tern.
THAWL – Rowlock pins.
TIER – A run of nets.
TIMBERS – Round branches or logs on which boats are pulled up the beach.
TOPPER – A marker rope.
TOWAN – A sand bank.
TREATH (TRAYTHE) – A rope, from pilchard seine to shore or beach (Cornish. Nance gives *treth*, a beach).
TRIGG – Ebb of the tide (Cornish. Nance gives Cornish *tryg).*
TUCK – Lifting the pilchards with a tuck-seine, and filling the boats.
UGGO – A sea cave.

See the faece 'n eyes ubb'm on the towan, did'ee?

John 'enery scat up that ol' gurry, didda ?

it the preens eckly can'ee ?

Sharkey's maed falled down on the caunce yes'day ... dear of 'er!

CADGWITH TODAY

Cadgwith is no longer the tightly-knit
Cornish fishing community of the past.
From the original cluster of thatched
cottages grouped around the cove,
modern bungalows and
houses continue to spread
over the surrounding hillsides.
Many of its thatched cottages, bought by Cadgwith
families when offered for sale by the Johnstone family in 1947, have since been sold,
for temptingly high prices, to incomers, often to become second homes. In summer it
is a thriving community, with a constant stream of visitors, who enjoy its beauty, its
gig racing, the noted singing at the Cadgwith Hotel, and its annual regatta; in winter,
when gales prevent net fishing, the cove becomes largely shuttered, silent and almost
deserted.

Pilchard seining is now history; with its decline the number of fishermen has
greatly decreased from fifty in 1889, to twenty six in 1976, thirteen in 1998, working
four boats double-handed, and five single-handed. Younger fishermen tend to fish from
Newlyn. In 2006 eight boats continued to work. A variety of fish are caught by nets,
and crabs, crayfish and lobster by pots, from April to December,

The use of the buildings continues to change; the old coastguard gig house is
now a shop, and the adjoining lifeboat house is the base for the Cadgwith Gig Club,
housing their gigs 'Buller', named after Richard 'Buller' Arthur, and 'Socoa'. Opposite
these are a crab shop, and the 'Crows Nest', a loft converted into an art and craft
gallery. 'Square Cellar' is now the 'Old Cellars Restaurant' owned by a Cadgwith man,
Mr L 'Sharkey' Stephens.

Yet with all these changes Cadgwith remains a very special place for most
Cornish folk, not only for its natural beauty and tranquillity but, with its small but
active fishing industry, a constant reminder of the great days of the pilchard seining
industry.

Old Coast Guard
Gig Hose on left.
Former Lifeboat
House on right
(Author)

REFERENCES

The Dwellings and people

1. Gover J *E Place names,* 1948, p580. Courtney Library, RIC.
2. Hitchens, F and Drew, S. *History of Cornwall, vol.ii,* 1824
3. *Per* Mr Henry Jane.
4. *Per* Mr Henry Jane
5. DDJ 340/3 CRO
6. DDJ 340/3 CRO
7. DDJ 340/5 CRO
8. DDJ 340/13 CRO
9. DDJ 340/7 CRO
10. DDJ 340/14 CRO
11. DDJ 340/15 CRO
12. DDJ 340/18 CRO
13. DDJ 340/1 CRO
14. DDJ 579/1 CRO
15. DDJ 340/16 CRO
16. *Per* Mr Tim Goddard (descendant)
17. *Grade Lands Survey Book.* S Davey Esq. MSS Transcribed 1855
18. *Kellys Post Office Directory of Cornwall* 1856
19. *Per* Mr R Buller Arthur
20. Johns Rev C A *A Week At The Lizard* 1848 p161
21. Vallentine R *Fisheries Of Cornwall Inspectors Reports.* MSS Courtney Library RIC
22. Cornwall Census Report 1851
23. *Kelly's Directory of Cornwall*
24. Douch H L Transcripts. Courtney Library, RIC
25. Cornwall Census 1871
26. DDJ1299 CRO
27. *Kelly's Post Office Directory of Cornwall* 1856
28. Tithe Apportionment 1841 CRO
29. *Per* Mrs Diana Low (descendant)
30. *Kelly's Post Office Directory of Cornwall* 1856
31. Cornwall Census 1871
32. Cornwall Census 1851
33. DDX 393/41-43 CRO
34. Gilbert C S *An historical survey of the County of Cornwall,* 1817-20.
35. *Royal Cornwall Gazette* 26.6.1846
36. *Royal Cornwall Gazette* 20.11.1878
37. Henderson C. *Ecclesiastical Antiquities* vol.1 225 Mss Courtney Library RIC
38. *Per* Canon Alan Dunstan
39. *Per* Henry Jane.

"Meat, Money…"

1. DDJ 1300 Cornwall Record Office
2. Lysons, Rev. D & S, *Magna Britannia, vol 3. Cornwall,* 1814, p280
3. *Cornishman* 19.6.1890
4. *Cornish Telegraph* 4.9.1863
5. Noall, C. *Cornish Seines and Seiners,* 1972
6. DDJ 1299 Cornwall Record Office
7. *Cornishman* 29.7.1880
8. *West Briton* 15.11.1839
9. Tangye, M *Cornish Archaeology* no. 35.1994
10. Nance, R Morton. *A glossary of Cornish Sea Words,* 1963, p36
11. Johns, Rev. C A *A week at the Lizard,* 1848 p113
12. Nance, R Morton *Ibid*
13. *Royal Cornwall Gazette* 21.1.1892
14. *West Briton* 17.9.1885 (Helston Supplement)
15. *West Briton* 12.10.1893
16. *West Briton* 7.9.1897
17. *Cornish Telegraph* 16.9.1909
18. *Cornubian* 24.9.1871
19. *Cornishman* 11.11.1880
20. *Cornish Telegraph* 9.1.1877
21. *Cornishman* 26.2.1880
22. Tangye, M *Fishing coves of the Lands End and the Lizard.* Ms.
23. *Per* Mr Henry Jane
24. *Cornish Telegraph* 23.11.1882
25. Nance, Morton R. *Ibid*
26. DDJ 1299. Cornwall Record Office
27. *Cornish Telegraph* 29.9.1870

Seines and Seiners

1. *Royal Cornwall Gazette* 10.8.1811
2. *Royal Cornwall Gazette* 1.11.1823
3. *Royal Cornwall Gazette* 16.4.1825
4. DDJ 1302 CRO
5. DDJ 1302 CRO
6. *West Briton* 13.11.1884
7. *West Briton* 29.10.1885 [Helston suppl.]
8. *Cornish Telegraph* 7.7.1881
9. *Cornish Telegraph* 28.7.1881
10. *Cornish Telegraph* 23.5.1876
11. *Cornish Telegraph* 30.10.1879
12. Per Mr. R. Buller Arthur 1972
13. Noall.C. *Cornish Seines and Seiners,* 1972. (No source quoted)
14. *West Briton* 12.10.1893
15. *West Briton* 6.8.1896
16. Vallentine, Rupert *Fisheries of Cornwall - Inspectors report,* 1896. Mss. Courtney library.
17. Per Mr R.Mitchell born 1900 (1975

Cadgwith)
18. *Royal Cornwall Gazette* 1897
19. *West Briton* 19.9.1901
20. *Cornish Telegraph* 24.11.1904
21. *West Briton* 28.11.1901
22. *Cornish Telegraph* 1.10.1908
23. *West Briton* 30.12.1842
24. *West Briton* 10.12.1874
25. Census report 1851
26. Per Mr.Henry Jane.

Cadgwith Whalers
1. *West Briton* 1.9.1843
2. *West Briton* 3.4.1863
3. *West Briton* 3.4.1863
4. *West Briton* 28.8.1863
5. *West Briton* 4.9.1863

Cellars, Lofts and Capstans
1. *West Briton* 17.11.1873
2. CRO DDJ 1299
3. Per Mr. Henry Jane
4. CRO DDJ 340/6
5. *Tithe Apportionment. Ruan Minor* 1841
6. Per Mr. Henry Jane
7. CRO DDJ 1299
8. CRO DDJ 1299
9. *Tithe Apportionment. Ruan Minor* 1841
10. CRO DDP 20/28/1&2 *Cadgwith Winch Committee Book* Aug 8 1913 - Oct 7 1930
11. CRO CDDJ 1300
12. CRO DDJ 579 (D) '*Western Rental Ledger*'
13. *West Briton* 17.9.1885 (Helston Supplement)
14. Per Mr. Henry Jane 1972
15. Per Mr. Henry Jane 1972
16. Per Mr. Henry Jane 1972
17. *Cornishman* 21.7.1887
18. *Grade Lands Survey Book*, S Davey Esq. Ms. per Anthony Unwin
19. *Cornishman* 16.6.1887
20. Per Mr. Henry Jane
21. *Cornish Telegraph* 5.5.1875
22. *West Briton* 29.08.1881
23. Per Mr. Henry Jane 1972
24. *Cornishman* 15.9.1881
25. *Cornish Telegraph* 9.1.1877
26. Per Mr. Henry Jane
27. *Royal Cornwall Gazette* 5.2.1864
28. Per Mr. R "Buller" Arthur
29. *Falmouth Cornubian* 7.1.1831

Barking Nets
1. *Cornish Telegraph* 17.2.1875
2. Vallentine, R. *Fisheries of Cornwall. Inspectors Report.* 1896. Ms, Courtney library RIC

The Todden
1 Information Mr Henry Jane
2 Information Mr R Buller Arthur

The Devil's Frying Pan
1. Courtney Library, Royal Institution of Cornwall
2. *Per* Dr Oliver Padel, Cambridge University (correspondence)
3. Henwood, G. *Mining Journal* supplement 27.6.1857
4. *Cornish Telegraph* 31.1.1851
5. *Directory of Penzance and its immediate neighbourhood for 1864.*

School Days and Recreation
1. DDJ 1302 CRO
2. *Royal Cornwall Gazette* 19.8.1859
3. *Royal Cornwall Gazette* 24.8.1860
4. *Census* 1861
5. Per Mrs. G. Hocking Ruan Minor Born 1902 (1982)
6. *Royal Cornwall Gazette* 4.5.1855
7. *Royal Cornwall Gazette* Jan. 1855
8. *Cornishman* 24.8.1882
9. *Royal Cornwall Gazette* 30.7.1868
10. *Cornish Telegraph* 28.9.1904
11. *West Briton* 14.6.1875
12. *West Briton* 13.8.1903
13. *West Briton* 11.6.1896
14. Per Mrs.G. Hocking Ruan Minor Born 1902 (1982)
15. Nance, R Morton *Folklore Recorded In The Cornish Language.* 1924
16. DDD/20/28/1 CRO

Smuggling

1. Borlase Rev. W *Parochial Memoranda 1740.* Mss Courtney Library, RIC
2. DDJ 2123 CRO
3. *Royal Cornwall Gazette* 4.8.1810
4. *Royal Cornwall Gazette* 18.2.1815
5. *Royal Cornwall Gazette* 24.2.1816
6. *Royal Cornwall Gazette* 15.3.1817
7. *Royal Cornwall Gazette* 26.1.1822
8. *West Briton* 14.10.1842
9. Roberts. J. *History of Constantine,* Mss 1929. Cornwall Centre
10. *West Briton* 2.4.1987

Wrecks and Wrecking

1. DDJ 340/17 CRO
2. *West Briton* 7.7.1826
3. *Royal Cornwall Gazette* 23.11.1838
4. *West Briton* 1.4.1839
5. *Royal Cornwall Gazette* 19.9.1867
6. *Royal Cornwall Gazette* 21.11.1867
7. *West Briton* 18.3.1869
8. *Cornishman* 11.9.1879
9. *Cornish Telegraph* 1.6.1893
10. *Royal Cornwall Gazette* 13.8.1858
11. *Royal Cornwall Gazette* 2.9.1809
12. DDJ 985 CRO
13. DDJ 985 CRO

Poltesco and Carleon Cove

1. Per Dr. Oliver Padel. Cambridge University
2. Henderson, Charles, Mss vol 6 p259. Courtney Library RIC
3. *Harrods Directory* 1878
4. *Kelly's Directory* 1856 and 1861
5. HH/7/62 Courtney Library RIC

Carleen Fish Cellars

6. Copy Courtney Library
7. Noall, C. *Cornish Seines and Seiners* (1972) p135 (no source given)
8. *West Briton* 18/5/1838
9. *West Briton* 4/9/1840
10. DDJ 1300 CRO

11. Tithe Appointment Grade 1841. CRO

Serpentine, Poltesco

12. *Cornish Telegraph* 8/6/1853
13. *Directory of Penzance* 1864
14. *Royal Cornwall Gazette* 11/9/1846
15. Hunt. Robert. '*Art Journal*' 1855 p258/60
16. *Royal Cornwall Gazette* 19/2/1847
17. *Cornish Telegraph* 2/5/1851
18. Jenkin Letter Book 1865 229 Courtney Library RIC
19. Hunt. Robert '*Art Journal*' 1855
20. *West Briton* 11/9/1876
21. *Cornish Telegraph* 21/12/1853
22. *Cornish Telegraph* 31/6/1851
23. *Cornish Telegraph* 13/10/1852
24. *Cornishman* 14/7/1883
25. Hunt. Robert '*Art Journal*' 1855
26. *Kelly's Directory* 1856
27. Census Report 1861
28. *Royal Cornwall Gazette* 3/5/1861
29. *West Briton* 25/10/1861
30. *Royal Cornwall Gazette* 11/11/1864
31. Jenkin Letter Book 22/9/1865 Index by R M Phillips. Courtney Library RIC
32. *Royal Cornwall Gazette* 7/8/1866
33. *West Briton* 24/1/1871
34. *West Briton* 11/9/1876
35. *West Briton* 31/8/1876
36. *West Briton* 11/9/1876
37. *Royal Cornwall Gazette* 26/7/1878
38. Boase, G C *Collectanea Cornubiensia* 1890
39. *Cornishman* 14/7/1883
40. *Royal Cornwall Gazette* 15/3/1866
41. *Cornishman* 14/7/1883
42. *Cornishman* 14/7/1883
43. *Cornishman* 14/7/1883
44. *Royal Cornwall Gazette* 3/11/1884
45. *West Briton* 20/5/1886, Supplement.
46. *West Briton* 22/5/1893
47. *West Briton* 4/5/1893
48. Information Mr Anthony H Unwin